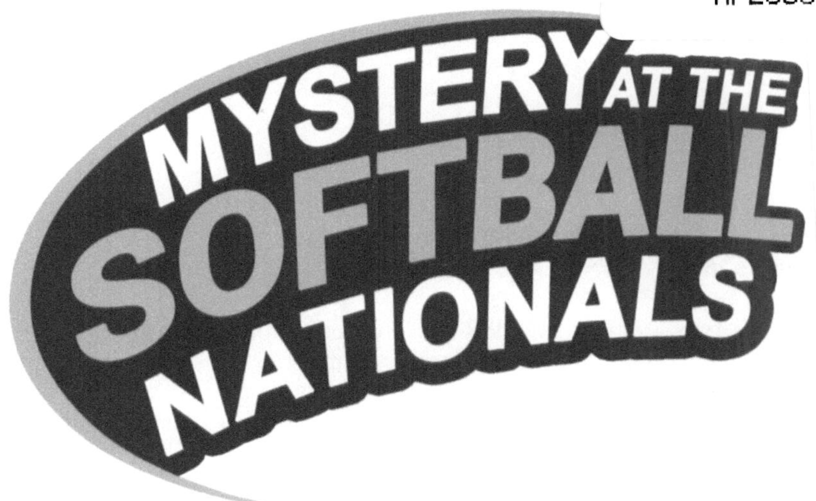

THOMAS LOCKHAVEN

2026

First Printing: 2026

ISBN 978-1-63911-209-8

Twisted Key Publishing, LLC
www.twistedkeypublishing.com

CONTENTS

CHAPTER 1
THE LAIR

7:17 P.M.

"You're sure they're not just sore losers?" Ava asked as her best friend Carol hung up her phone.

Ava plopped down on the sofa, kicked off her black Converse high-top sneakers, and tucked her feet underneath her.

The girls were in their secret headquarters, The Lair, otherwise known as Ava's parents' basement. The Lair had been repurposed as the girls' crime laboratory and podcasting studio.

"Doubtful," said Carol, hopping onto the couch beside her. "You heard Coach Brier. They were on a fourteen-game winning streak, and suddenly, they lost to the Red Rockets twice. A team they'd easily beaten in the past." She made a face that teetered between doubtful and highly unlikely.

"Maybe the pressure got to them, or maybe the Red Rockets have improved," suggested Ava. "I mean, if you play the same team over and over, they're gonna learn how to compete against you."

"Yes, but Coach Brier said she had a *feeling* in her gut that something wasn't right." The tone of Carol's voice said she believed her.

"So do I after eating too many tacos," Ava countered.

"Aves," said Carol wearily. "I think we should *at least* watch the video of their last game against the Rockets. Besides, Becky Adams, who just *happens* to be their pitcher, is our friend." She tilted her head, raising an eyebrow. "We owe it to her."

"That's *so* unfair," sighed Ava, hugging a pillow. "You *know* I have a weakness for friendship."

"And tacos." Carol smiled. "It's a curse to care about your friends," she continued, "work through the pain."

"Easy for you to say, you have no friends," Ava muttered.

Carol's phone began vibrating across a coffee table, which Ava had stolen from her parents' living room. "That's probably the coach sending us the link."

"That, or your phone's possessed," yawned Ava. "You know what the *real* crime is…?"

Carol stared at Ava in bored anticipation, drumming her fingers on her leg.

"Never mind." Ava looked away with a dramatic sigh. "I can tell you're not interested."

"I am," Carol replied, swiping her index finger across her phone screen. She turned and looked at her friend suspiciously. "Is this going to be something I regret? Am I enabling *bad* behavior?"

"No." Ava narrowed her eyes. "Maybe."

"Alright, out with it. What was your *deep* thought?"

"I was *simply* going to say that I was surprised *they*—being the organization that hires musicians for sporting events—haven't invited you to perform the national anthem at one of their softball games, or… *any* game for that matter."

"Because the bassoon is the first instrument that comes to mind when you think of a solo performance at a softball game," Carol said, making a face.

"Cheng Yu, your archnemesis, played 'Anti-Hero' by Taylor Swift on the xylophone at the last game." Ava paused, letting her thoughts drift away to the performance. "It was breathtaking. Exhilarating." She waited a beat. "Think of the exposure."

"I'm thinking of something right now," said Carol, eyeing a pillow, "and it starts with *suffocation*. And Cheng Yu, by the way, is *not* my archnemesis. It's Odessa March. Cheng Yu is… insignificant—she's a percussionist."

"Oh, right. Odessa is the oboist, with the magical fingers." Ava laughed, wriggling her fingers at Carol. "Not my words, of course. I'm simply quoting the Livingston local news."

"Are you finished?" asked Carol, fingers inching across the sofa toward a pillow.

"That depends," said Ava, "are you perturbed?"

"Perturbed, disturbed, literally *all* of the *urbed* words."

"Then my work here is done." Ava pantomimed brushing off her hands. "I suggest we watch the video Coach Brier sent us." She snatched up the remote and turned the television on.

With an audible sigh, Carol synced her phone with the television and clicked the video link from Coach Brier.

"At least we're watching softball and not golf," said Ava.

"Or curling," Carol replied. "*There's* a real adrenaline-driven sport."

"Can you imagine?" Ava giggled. "Mom. Dad. I aspire to be a curler. I shall travel to the ends of the earth in search of a true master to teach me the art of curling."

"When you retire, you could write a bestselling novel," Carol suggested. "Pushing Stones, a bestselling novel, *guaranteed* to put you to sleep."

Ava smiled, nodding, picturing herself as a bestselling author. "Your words are steeped in wisdom, Big Brain. I'll take your suggestion under consideration and have my people get back with your people." Ava shook Carol's hand to solidify the deal.

"Alright," said Carol, turning her attention to the television. "The video's loaded and ready to go. Let's see what the coach sent."

"Fair enough," said Ava, settling into the sofa. "So, according to our conversation with Coach

Brier, each team has a series of hand signals for the type of pitch that's about to be thrown."

"Right." Carol nodded. "There are hand signals for the fastball, changeup, drop, curve, screw, and rise—plus a few other variations that Becky, the pitcher, is working on."

"Sheesh." Ava gave Carol an impressed look. "Someone's been doing their homework."

"Rote memorization." Carol shrugged. "When you're gifted, it just comes naturally."

"*Sooo* modest." Ava laughed.

"Thank you for noticing." Carol smiled.

"So, if the opposing team knew the other team's signals, they would know what type of pitch was coming—making it much easier for the batter to hit."

"Oh yeah, they would have a considerable advantage." Carol gave a quick nod.

Ava thought for a moment. "Isn't it the catcher who sends the signal to the pitcher?"

Carol nodded.

"So, how would the batter know what pitch is being called if her back is to the catcher? She can't see the catcher's signal."

"It would have to be a team effort," said Carol. "Someone would have to see the catcher's signal to the pitcher—and then somehow clue the batter in as to what pitch is about to be thrown."

"Why not change the signals each game?" asked Ava. "Seems like a simple fix."

"They might already do that; we'll have to ask Coach Brier what their protocol is. I know that at their level, there are dozens of different plays and variations on each pitch—it's a lot to memorize."

"Yeah, I'm sure," Ava agreed. "Alright, I think I understand enough to know what I'm looking for."

Carol pressed the play button on the remote. "Watch for *anything* out of the ordinary," she said as the game jumped to life on the television.

On the screen, an athletic girl wearing a red baseball cap and a white uniform with red piping crouched over home plate. She tapped her bat on her foot and then eyed the pitcher. The catcher dropped her hand between her knees and lowered two fingers, then one, then three.

"There's the signal to the pitcher," said Carol.

Ava nodded, eyes locked on the screen.

The player settled in, bat cocked above her shoulder. Suddenly the batter swung. There was a crisp *crack*. The ball rocketed off the bat. The camera swooped around, following the trajectory of the ball as it flew deep into centerfield. The batter rounded first and easily made it to second. The camera whipped back around as her teammate, who had been on third base, slid into home in a cloud of dust, scoring.

"That was a great hit!" Carol exclaimed.

The camera repositioned, displaying home base as a new player stepped into the batter's box. She tugged at her helmet, tapped the bat on the ground, and stared down the pitcher.

The catcher signaled. The batter waited, and then the catcher signaled again. The batter stepped out of the box, rolling her shoulders, adjusting her helmet.

"Pause it for a second," said Ava, watching closely. "So, let me get this straight. The catcher sent her signal to the pitcher—"

"The pitcher didn't like the call," added Carol.

"So the catcher gave her a different call."

"Right." Carol gave a quick nod.

The batter stepped back from the plate, wiped her forehead, and then tapped her bat on the ground a couple times. She looked up toward the pitcher and then repositioned herself in the batter's box.

"Do they reset every time they make a new call?" asked Ava. "Because that could be something."

"I guess," Carol agreed. "I have no idea. Softball players have a lot of little rituals."

"Yeah, but that little ritual could be a code…" said Ava. "Maybe we should take note of any peculiarities we see. You know, excessive bat tapping or hand motions."

"Good idea." Carol nodded. "We'll see if we can spot any patterns."

The batter crouched, waiting for the pitch. The ball came in low with a heavy spin. The player widened her stance, sank, and came up under the ball. Another solid hit. The camera smoothly followed the ball as it flew deep into the outfield, bouncing off the wall.

"Wow! I can see why Coach Brier is worried," said Ava. "This team is *really* good."

Carol nodded, a frown forming on her face. "It's frustrating being limited to one vantage point."

"What do you mean?" asked Ava.

"All we can see is the batter, umpire, and catcher," Carol complained. "I'm not sure how helpful this video is going to be."

"Yeah," agreed Ava. "We need a wide shot where we can see all of the players, the dugout, the coaches, and the crowd. Anyone could be sending them signals."

"Exactly," Carol agreed.

"Plus," Ava continued, "we're missing out on the true experience; shouldn't we be scarfing down hot dogs and soda while we watch the video?"

Carol dug in her pocket and pulled out a box of raisins and dumped a warm, sticky clump into Ava's hand. "Use your imagination."

"I have so many questions," Ava sighed.

"Maybe we'll get lucky and they'll reposition the camera," said Carol.

"Doubtful," said Ava, rubbing the raisins from her hand onto the coffee table.

A heavyset girl jogged into the batter's box. She ran a forearm across her forehead, spat, and then lined up at the plate. The catcher flashed a quick series of hand signals—three fingers, one finger, three fingers. The batter looked down for a brief second, readjusted her sweatband, and then eyed the pitcher. Seconds later, there was a roar from the crowd as the girl smacked the ball into oblivion.

"It's like déjà vu with each player," said Ava.

"Yep." Carol fast-forwarded through the video, stopping here and there, checking for a change in camera angle.

"They're not going to move it," said Ava. "We'll need to think of something else."

"I'm going to call the coach," said Carol.

CHAPTER 2
THE PLAN

Coach Brier picked up on the second ring. Carol put the phone on speaker so Ava could hear the conversation.

"Hi, Coach Brier, this is Carol and Ava. I've got you on speaker."

"Hi, Carol. Hi, Ava, did you guys find anything on the video?" Her voice a mix of excitement and hope.

"Not yet," said Carol, "we're still reviewing the game."

"I see…"

Ava pictured the coach's excitement deflating like a balloon.

"Our final game is tomorrow night," Coach Brier's voice was tense. "This is a team that we've won against consistently… it just doesn't make sense."

"We understand," Carol reassured her. "The video is helpful, but it only shows a limited view."

"We need to observe the players, the coaches and the audience," explained Ava. "If your signs *are* being stolen, we need to find out who is relaying that information to the batter, and how."

"I understand," Coach Brier sighed. "I really waited too long to say anything."

Carol felt bad for her, especially for their friend Becky, but the coach was right, she should have contacted them earlier if she felt cheating was involved.

"How much do you guys know about softball?" Coach Brier asked.

"About as much as I know about igneous rocks," said Ava.

"That's tough," said Coach Brier.

"We're fast learners though," said Carol, giving Ava the stink eye. "What do you have in mind?"

"I was thinking about bringing you to the game tomorrow as team assistants," said Coach Brier.

"Undercover." Ava's eyes glazed as she rubbed her hands together.

"But," Coach Brier continued, "you need at least a *basic* understanding of the game. Have either of you ever played?"

"No," said Carol, "but trust me, we can do a deep dive—watch some YouTube videos—"

"I just remembered," said Coach Brier, "aren't you guys friends with Becky Adams? No one can know who you are and why you are there."

"Yes," said Carol, "we know Becky, but that isn't a deal breaker," she assured her. "We're professionals. I promise you, when you see us, you won't recognize us."

"Won't we need uniforms?" asked Ava.

"That's the easiest part," said Coach Brier. "I'll take care of that." She hesitated for a moment before continuing. "I can't begin to say how important this is—and I understand that much of this is my fault."

"The important thing is you're doing something about it," Carol reassured her.

"You're right." Coach Brier paused again, clearly struggling with her decision. "Okay, the game is tomorrow night at seven at the Parker Stadium Complex."

Ava quickly typed the information into her phone while the coach spoke.

"Meet me tomorrow at Willow Oaks High School at four? Main entrance."

"We'll be there," said Carol.

"Perfect, I'll have everything ready for you."

"Coach," Ava chimed in. "Can you email us a list of all the players? That way we can begin combing through social media profiles to see if we can find anything."

"It'll allow us to cross-reference players from the Red Rockets team to see if any of the girls are friends with any of the girls from your team," Carol explained.

"That's a great idea!" said Coach Brier. "I'll email their information to you."

"I have to ask," said Carol. "Any idea as to why players would risk so much by cheating?"

"At this level, the girls are playing for a *lot* more than a tournament trophy. There will be scouts from *top* universities there. Some of the scholarships are worth hundreds of thousands of dollars."

"Hundreds of thousands of dollars?" mouthed Ava. "Sorry, Carol, you're on your own. I'm quitting detective work and taking up softball."

"That's definitely a powerful motive," Carol agreed, thinking aloud.

"It's a *lot* of pressure," said Coach Brier. "It would be a shame for these girls to work so hard, only to have it *stolen* away from them."

"We understand," said Ava softly, empathizing with her. "If someone is cheating, we'll catch them." A soft beep sounded on the other line.

"I've got to go," said Coach Brier quickly. "Tina, the assistant coach, is calling me. I'll send you the player roster. It has everything you'll need on it. Let me know if you have more questions."

"We will," Carol assured her.

The girls said goodbyes and hung up the phone.

"You know what this means." Carol smiled excitedly.

"Disguises," Ava trilled. She hopped to her feet. "I'll give Kaitlyn a call."

Carol's phone buzzed, she glanced at the screen and nodded. "Wow, Coach Brier is like *super-efficient*. She just sent me the team roster."

"That's fast," Ava agreed.

"I'll shoot you an email with the attachment," said Carol. "We can divide up the players into two groups."

"Perfect," said Ava as she scrolled through her contacts for Kaitlyn's number. "We should probably grab some snacks. It's going to be a long night."

CHAPTER 3
INCOGNITO

10:35 A.M. Mane Attraction Salon

Kaitlyn pulled Ava's hair back in a tight pony. Her usual light brown hair streaked with purple highlights was now a golden honeysuckle blonde.

Ava adjusted a pair of blue-framed glasses on her nose and smiled at Carol, displaying a set of fake braces.

Kaitlyn's expertly applied makeup and contouring had transformed Ava into a completely different person.

"Geez," gushed Carol, praising Kaitlyn's artistic abilities, "she looks amazing."

Kaitlyn took a step back admiring her work. "She does, doesn't she? I don't think your own mother will recognize you."

"Kaitlyn, you're a magician!" exclaimed Ava, staring into the mirror. "And you…" She shook her head, staring at Carol in disbelief. "If I passed by you on the sidewalk, I wouldn't recognize you. Well, except for your oversized head."

"Her head isn't oversized," laughed Kaitlyn.

"Pfft," laughed Ava. She gave Kaitlyn a you-know-what-I'm-talking-about look.

"My head is perfectly proportional to the rest of my body." Carol balled up her face, giving Ava the stink eye.

"Of course it is. I mean, I'm *sure* that's what they told the T-Rex: 'Don't you listen to those mean dinosaurs, your arms are just the right size for your body. Now touch your toes.'"

"I think we set her up for that one," snickered Kaitlyn.

"Unfortunately," agreed Carol.

"Besides the size of Carol's cranium, what do you think about the makeover?" Kaitlyn smiled.

Ava carefully studied her best friend. Her strawberry-blonde hair was now a light brown, streaked with golden highlights. Her freckles had vanished under Kaitlyn's makeup brush, but the most startling change was her eyes. Carol had what Ava called Windex-blue eyes. Now, thanks to colored contacts, they were brown.

"You look great, Firefly, I mean it!"

The door chimed and a young woman stepped inside the salon; she gave a quick wave to Kaitlyn and then turned her attention to the shelves stocked with hair and beauty products.

"Hi, Bethany," Kaitlyn chirped. "I'll be right with you." She turned her attention back to the girls, pointing a finger at them. "*Details*. I want *all* the juicy details when you solve this case!"

"We promise we'll fill you in with all the *sordid* details!" Carol grinned, giving Kaitlyn a quick hug.

Ava leaned in and gave Kaitlyn a quick hug, and then another. "The second one was for London. Please tell her we said hello!"

"I will." Kaitlyn smiled. "She'll be disappointed that she missed you."

Ava's eyes slid over to a picture of Kaitlyn's daughter. The year before, they helped solve a case and then used the reward money to cover the cost of a surgery that allowed London to hear. Once quiet and withdrawn, London's personality had blossomed. Kaitlyn said she was making up for lost time.

"We'll come see her soon!" Carol promised.

"You better!" Kaitlyn laughed, playfully shooing the girls out the door. She turned and motioned for Bethany to join her at the wash and rinse station as the door closed behind them.

CHAPTER 4
DERIK IS SO CONFUSED

11:52 Main Street Diner

Derik stood in the middle of the busy diner looking confused. He brushed a mop of blond hair from his forehead and checked his phone again. Yep, sure enough, the message read, *Last booth, by the kitchen.* He eyed the last booth suspiciously; there were two girls sitting at the table, but neither looked like Ava or Carol.

"Derik is looking at us *dubiously*," giggled Carol. She caught his eye, winked at him, and motioned him over.

"Must you fawn over him?" Ava rolled her eyes.

Derik flipped his bangs with a toss of his head, revealing a mischievous blue eye as he made his way over.

"He's going to give himself whiplash," said Ava. "Maybe you should suggest he make a small investment in scissors."

"Oh my God." He looked from Ava to Carol. "I would have never realized it was you!"

"All thanks to Kaitlyn," said Ava, brushing a hand through her hair with a flourish.

"I ordered you a cheeseburger," said Carol, "with tots."

"Thanks, you guys look amazing," he gushed, settling into the bench across from them.

"So what you're saying is, we didn't look amazing before?" Ava sighed.

Derik shook his head and wiggled a finger. "No way I'm falling for that. You guys have trained me too well—besides," he said coyly, "you *always* look amazing. Except for that time…" Derik pretended to stare off into space, tapping his chin with his finger, contemplating.

"Ohhh, someone just got burned." Carol patted Ava's shoulder. "Do you want me to rub some aloe on that little heart of yours?"

"You do realize that Derik said *I* always look amazing. Emphasis on the *I*." Ava smiled. "Perhaps there's something *you two* need to discuss. I'll look the other way if it's too uncomfortable."

Derik coughed politely. "So, Carol, brown eyes huh?" He stared at her for a beat too long.

Carol fidgeted in her seat, feeling a blush coming on. "I know, right?"

"She was going to wear a hat as part of her disguise, but unfortunately, we couldn't find one to fit her head."

"I know, they were all too big," Carol smirked.

"Oh, nice comeback." Ava looked impressed. "I still think you need to work on your comedic delivery; it's all about timing."

"You two squabble like sisters," said Derik. "What a strange word… squabble."

"A noisy quarrel about something petty, or trivial," Carol said, glancing up from her phone.

"Firefly." Ava's hand swept to her heart. "I believe Derik just implied that our conversations were petty and trivial. I, for one, am insulted."

"Oh brother," Derik sighed.

The trio paused their verbal dueling long enough to allow the waitress to serve their food. And then, as usual, Carol, being the voice of reason, slowly guided the conversation toward discussing the case.

"Thanks for agreeing to meet with us," Carol began. "This case is a little bit out of our wheelhouse."

"Not a problem at all," said Derik, taking a sip of water. "I love helping you guys. Anything you need."

"Thanks." Carol smiled and patted his hand.

Ava looked away, suddenly feeling awkward.

"We'll need help researching the girls' online presence—Instagram, TikTok. Counting both teams and coaches, there are over forty people—maybe more."

"Oof. That is a massive list," said Derik, "especially if they have multiple social media profiles and lots of followers."

"It's a lot," agreed Carol. "That's why we really need your help."

"It's all good." Derik smiled. "I'll create a spreadsheet so we can cross-reference everyone."

"Carol said that you were able to score some tickets to the game?" asked Ava.

Derik nodded and held up a finger, finishing his bite. "Yep, I scored a couple."

"How did you manage to do that?" Ava asked. "Coach Brier said the game sold out months ago."

"My dad's bank helped finance that stadium. We always get premium tickets," said Derik, wiping his mouth with a napkin. "I'll be able to watch for any *facinorous* activities." He grinned, wiggling his fingers.

"That's great," said Carol. "Nice having a dad that knows everyone in town."

"Also, nice use of the word *facinorous*," said Ava. "I have absolutely no idea what it means, but…"

"It means wicked," explained Carol.

"Oh, well done you." Ava smiled.

"The more eyes we can have on the field, the better," said Carol. "It's going to be incredibly hard figuring out who the cheaters are. It could really be anyone. A parent, a player, a coach."

"Or, no one at all," added Ava.

"Wait, even Coach Brier could be a suspect?" Derik asked, surprised.

"I've seen stranger things," said Ava. "Coach Brier could be using this opportunity to divert attention away from herself. Someone could be paying her big money to throw the game."

"It happens all the time in professional sports," said Carol.

"That's horrible," said Derik.

"There have also been a *lot* of cases where the person who committed the crime became involved in the investigation," Carol explained. "They act like they're trying to help the police, when they're really trying to steer them astray."

"Plus, as an added bonus, it helps the wrongdoer find out *what* the police know," said Ava.

"Makes sense." Derik dipped his hamburger into a blob of ketchup and took a bite.

Ava slid a stack of napkins over to him. "You're leaking, Count Dracula."

"Thank you," said Derik, grabbing a napkin from the stack.

Ava glanced over at Carol, who was chewing on her bottom lip, a habit she'd had since grade school. Ava teased her that one day she'd chew her lip off and they'd replace it with a giant gummy bear—a green one. She'd be one ninety-ninth Hulk.

"Ah," said Carol suddenly, "*something* just hit me."

"Tempting…" Ava cracked her knuckles. "Do tell."

"It all comes down to the batter," Carol continued.

"Are you talking about your chicken or softball?" Ava joked.

"Funny," smirked Carol, snatching a napkin from the stack. She snagged a pen from her crossbody bag.

"Here's home base." She drew a circle on the napkin. "Here's the rest of the field." She made a tear-shaped drawing that connected with home plate. "The batter stands here"—she tapped the napkin—"the pitcher here."

Derik and Ava nodded that they understood.

"So, the batter *only* has this triangular, pie-slice wedge as her line of sight," Carol explained. "*That's* where we need to look to find our cheaters. They have to be able to see the catcher's call signs. *Boom.*"

Carol let her pen fall onto the table dramatically—only to have it roll onto the floor where it was promptly stepped on.

Ava stared at the pen for a moment, and then gave Carol a look of disappointment. "Thank you for your remedial drawing. Sure, it looks easy on that tiny napkin," she expounded, "but that wedge encompasses *all* the players, the coach, and the spectators. So you're talking about *hundreds* of people."

Derik nodded in agreement. "It could be some dude sitting in the audience with binoculars, and when a pitch is called he sends the information to the coach and the coach sends the call to the batter. We would just have to figure out *how*."

"There could literally be dozens of ways the other team is cheating," said Carol.

"Don't fret, D-Man, it's a good idea." Ava paused, eyeing Derik. "Is it alright if I call you D-Man? It sort of just rolls off the tongue. Try it."

Out of the corner of her eye, Ava could see Carol mouthing D-Man. Derik winced as if he'd just eaten bad fish.

"Maybe not," Ava concluded. "It's a work in progress." She took a beat to gather her thoughts. "I don't think—"

Derik eyed Carol.

She waved Derik's look aside. "Too easy."

"I don't believe," said Ava, starting again, "that there's enough time for someone in the audience to see the sign, interpret it, signal the coach, and then have the coach signal the batter. Isn't it just a matter of seconds before the pitch is thrown?"

"Not sure," said Carol. "It is a good point, though."

"We could test the theory," said Derik. "I'm sure that with practice, they could get it down to a few seconds."

"What if someone in the audience were to hold up a sign that lets the batter know what's being thrown," Carol suggested. "You know, cut out the middleman. Then the batter only has to look up at the person in the crowd."

"Yeah." Derik nodded. "They could have a code. Fastball could be a rocket or a bullet. Curve ball could be a snake."

The trio looked up as the waiter dropped off the check.

"I guess it could happen, I mean think about it, our entire generation communicates through emojis. It's quick and easy." Carol drummed her fingers on the table. "Honestly, we're going to have to figure this one out on the fly."

"High pressure is how we roll," said Derik, taking a swig from his drink.

"How we *roll*?" Ava sighed. "The only thing I want to roll right now is my eyes."

"If you were a pirate, you could roll your R's," suggested Carol.

"Speaking of pirates," said Derik with a hint of mischief in his eyes. "And this is a *true* fact that I learned in school last week," he assured them. "Do you know why it takes pirates so long to learn the alphabet?" Ava and Carol looked at each other and then shrugged in tandem.

"Because they spend *years* at C." Derik cracked up at the ridiculousness of his own joke.

"That's horrible," moaned Carol. She balled up a napkin and threw it at him. "You pay the bill. That was *awful*."

"It was worth it." Derik smiled, accepting his fate.

"We need a horrible joke jar," said Ava, "and every time someone says a bad joke, they put a quarter in the jar."

"Makes cents," said Derik. "Get it? Because it's a quarter?"

"We're going to be so rich," Carol sighed.

"Yeah." Derik nodded begrudgingly. "I heard it." He reached into his pocket and put a five-dollar bill on the table. "I'm hoping that will get me through the week."

"Doubtful," laughed Ava. "Doubtful."

CHAPTER 5
SOUL CRUSHERS

3:37 P.M. Willow Oaks High School

"I look like a skinny fluorescent banana," said Ava, eyeing herself in the girls' locker room mirror. "All I need is a Dole sticker on my forehead."

Carol joined Ava in front of the mirror. "Your uniform goes great with your blonde hair."

"Really?" Ava brushed her bangs from her face and tilted her head to the side. "I guess you're right." She adjusted her top and fidgeted with the waistline of her pants. "I never knew these uniforms were so stretchy."

"I could sleep in them," said Carol, pulling her hair through the back of her baseball cap. "By the way, I *love* the name of our team." She smiled.

"The *Soul Crushers*," the girls laughed.

"Let's hope it's not a self-fulfilling prophecy," said Carol.

"Every time I hear that phrase, I hear Mrs. Chang, our English teacher, in my head: 'Whether you think you can or think you can't, you're right.'"

"Henry Ford." Carol nodded. "One of my favorite visionaries." She made a fist and tapped her chest twice with it. "Assembly-line innovation. *Respect.*"

"Okay…" Ava eyed her friend curiously. "It's the Wright brothers for me. They hoofed up a giant sand dune, climbed onto a flimsy airplane made of wood and canvas, and then said to each other, 'Hey, let's jump.' They *literally* risked their lives for progress."

"Yeah, true," Carol agreed. "Oh my gosh, you know what I just realized, both of our favorite historical figures had something to do with transportation. Coincidence? I think not."

"Speaking of transportation," said Ava, glancing at her watch, "we gotta get to the bus."

She threw what *appeared* to be an ordinary backpack over her shoulder. However, unlike most teens, her backpack contained a portable crime lab filled with all of the necessary components they would need for an investigation.

Carol shrugged her backpack over her shoulders and adjusted the straps. "History is filled with a lot of amazing people, doing amazing things. It's so inspiring."

"Yeah," Ava hesitated, wishing she could share Carol's enthusiasm. "I wish I were feeling a little more inspired right now. For the first time in a *long* time, I'm really worried about solving a case. People's futures are *depending* on us."

"You're talking about college scouts and scholarships?"

Ava nodded.

"Aves." Carol threw an arm over her best friend's shoulder. "We've solved over a dozen cases; this one won't be any different."

"Yeah, I know." Ava nodded. "I just feel out of my element, you know what I mean? Neither of us knows much about softball. It's going to be incredibly hard to figure out how they're cheating. This is the championships—they don't get another chance." She looked at Carol and gave her a wan smile. "No pressure, right?"

"Look, this case is no harder than any other case we've solved," said Carol. "Remember when Mr. Willis taught us to take complex word problems and break them into their simplest elements?"

"Of course," said Ava. "He pounded it into our heads. I now know *everything* I need to know about speed, time, and distance related to train travel."

"Exactly! Which, by the way, will be *great* the next time we decide to take a trip across the country on a train." Carol bumped Ava's shoulder as they headed for the exit.

"We just need to follow his advice and break down the components of the case," Carol continued, "just like we would a word problem. Who knows the call signs? Who can see the signals given by the catcher? Who is deciphering the calls and communicating with the batter?"

"That makes sense," Ava agreed.

"Once we have the answers to those questions, then we can turn the case into a big math problem."

"Great," Ava sighed. "You just figured out how to turn crime-solving into my least favorite subject."

"I'm slowly trying to suck the life out of you, so I can grow more powerful," laughed Carol. She did a double bicep flex and then threw her shoulder into the locker room door; it swung open, thudding against the frame.

Ava shook her head and sighed. "You bruised your shoulder, didn't you?"

"Yep." Carol winced. "Big time."

The girls hurried down a short hallway and exited the side of the school into the parking lot.

"Noticed you didn't shoulder that door open," teased Ava.

The girls raised their hands over their eyes, protecting them from the bright sunlight. Coach Brier was standing in front of a yellow school bus, surrounded by excited parents. Girls dressed in neon yellow uniforms were grabbing duffel bags and gear out of the back of their parents' cars.

"It's like a parking lot filled with glow sticks," whispered Ava.

Coach Brier made eye contact with Ava and Carol as they approached. She excused herself and broke away from the parents. Another woman wearing jeans and a neon yellow *Soul Crushers* hoodie became the new target for the parents as they swarmed around her.

"Coach," a girl's voice rang across the parking lot. Coach Brier held up a finger, signaling to the girl that she would be with her in a minute.

"I can't get over how different you look. You *are* Ava and Carol?" She gave them a tight smile.

The girls smiled, pleased with their disguises.

"I'm introducing you to the team as assistants in training. I'll explain that you're here to learn the ropes, so to speak."

"Got it." Carol nodded.

"Not me," said Ava. "I'm unclear as to what an assistant does, besides the obvious, *assisting*."

"Anything and everything," said Coach Brier. "You'll be helping the girls with loading and carrying equipment, stretching—if they need water, you'll grab them water—whatever they need."

"Stretching?" Ava gave a worried smile.

"Don't worry." Coach Brier scrunched up her nose in a failed attempt to smile. "You'll be fine."

"I can already feel the abuse clawing its way up my back to my shoulders," said Ava.

Carol gave her a look, then turned back to the coach. "I'm sure we'll figure things out," she assured her. "I know you have to get back to your team, but I have a couple questions—before things get too hectic."

"Fire away," said Coach Brier, waving another player away while simultaneously glancing at her watch.

"Who has access to the call signs?" asked Carol.

"Good question. Everyone *used* to have access." She looked wearily over her shoulder at the bus. "That all changed when we suspected something was amiss. Now only a few *select* players have wristbands with all of the signs—Tina and I have a master call sheet with them as well."

"That's Tina, the assistant coach, right?" Carol nodded toward the bus. "The one that is currently being swarmed?"

"Yes." Coach Brier quickly stole a look at the assistant coach and then turned back to the girls. "Unfortunately, I need to help her. The players are like hyenas. Soon they'll drag her away, never to be seen again."

"That's brutal," exclaimed Ava.

Coach Brier nodded. "That's girls softball for you. I'm sorry to throw you into the fray, but in order for my team to believe you're assistants, you're going to have to act like assistants—and right now, that means loading the bus." She gave the girls her infamous tight smile. "Don't worry, I'll be able to answer your questions once we're settled in."

"Fair enough," said Ava.

"Come on, I'll introduce you to the hyenas—I mean girls."

Coach Brier blew her whistle and motioned the team over. The players dropped what they were doing and hustled over, circling around the coach.

"Glad my mom's not here," whispered Ava. "If she saw how effective that whistle is, it would be the end of my freedom. *Whistle. Whistle.* Do your laundry. *Whistle. Whistle.* Feed the cat."

"You don't have a cat."

"She'd buy a cat just as an excuse to use the whistle. Never underestimate the power of the whistle, Carol." Ava gave her a knowing look.

Coach Brier held her hand up, and the group fell silent, reinforcing Ava's deepest fears. This woman should never meet her mother. She glanced at Becky, who eyed her disinterestedly.

To Becky, they were just a couple of teens that had little to do with her game tonight. Their disguises were working perfectly.

"Everyone, this is Marla and Sammi. They'll be working as assistants tonight." Ava and Carol waved awkwardly to the team.

"I want you guys," she said, pointing to the team, "to focus on the game. Sammi and Marla will handle the grunt work." This brought smiles to the girls' faces.

"Yes!" said a girl with arms like a lumberjack.

Carol stared at her heavily muscled shoulders; she looked like she could carry all of the team's gear herself—including the bus.

"Great enthusiasm, Kara." Coach Brier smiled. The rest of the team laughed. "She plays first base and centerfield," the coach explained to Ava and Carol. "We call her the intimidator."

"Understandable," muttered Carol under her breath.

Ava shot her a thumbs-up. "Respect."

"*Awkward*," Carol whispered to Ava.

"Alright!" yelled Coach Brier. "We leave in fifteen!" She patted the front of the school bus. "Load her up!"

"That's our cue," said Ava, tapping Carol's shoulder.

The girls busied themselves, lugging coolers and duffel bags across the parking lot and loading them onto the bus. The players who were a few years older mostly ignored Ava and Carol—other than to lug equipment over and drop it in a pile at their feet.

Becky handed Carol a heavy duffel bag without so much as giving her a second glance.

Carol would have to thank Kaitlyn again for her tremendous job with their disguises. She watched as Becky joined a small group of girls she recognized from their pictures on the Soul Crushers webpage: Lilly, the other pitcher, and the two catchers. Each of the girls had a yellow band around their wrist.

"Did you notice the wristband?" Carol asked Ava when the girls had a moment alone.

"Yep, they must be the *chosen few* that get the call signs."

"It's going to make—" Carol stopped talking when a tall girl—her head shaved on one side, and cut in a blue bob on the other—approached them.

"Hussle up, it's time to go." She jerked her head to the side toward the door of the bus and walked away.

A puff of blue-gray smoke coughed from the exhaust as the bus shuddered as if waking up from a deep sleep.

"That's Meredith." Carol winked. "Third base. She likes piano, ice sculpting, death metal, and long walks on the beach."

"Lovely." Ava smiled as they boarded the bus. "I like the Doctor Jekyll and Mr. Hyde thing she has going on with her hair."

"Always good to have options." Carol smiled back at her as they made their way down the narrow aisle to the rear of the bus.

CHAPTER 6
PARKER STADIUM COMPLEX

5:07 P.M.

"I think we should ask for a raise," Ava whispered as the girls tromped noisily off the bus. "Not only are we doing detective work, but we've been sneakily conned into performing *arduous* manual labor. I want to renegotiate my contract."

"A little hard work never hurt anyone," Carol replied with a shrug.

"Tell that to all of the gymnasts who suffer with white lung."

"There's no such thing as *white* lung." Carol rolled her eyes.

"Yes there is," Ava insisted, "it's from chalk dust."

Carol gave Ava a look that said *here we go again*.

"Have you seen those huge clouds of dust erupting from gymnasts' hands when they smack them together?" Ava smacked her palms together. "It's like Mount Vesuvius."

"Amazing." Carol yawned, fishing her phone from her pocket.

"Our beloved teachers," Ava added dramatically. "Think how much chalk dust they inhale every year. Probably several tons."

"Woah." Carol nodded, staring at her phone. "I can't believe you're right. White lung does exist… incredible."

"You see, true knowledge comes from here"—Ava pointed to her heart—"not here." She moved her hand to her head.

"How about next time Mount Vesuvius is active, you climb it?" Carol suggested. "You know, get a bird's-eye view?"

"Will they let you do that?"

"Of course. Of course." Carol nodded emphatically. "They *encourage* it." She smacked Ava on the back.

"Cool." Ava grinned. "Something to think about."

"Yep." Carol grinned. "Now, come on, this bus isn't going to unload itself."

"Alright." Ava sighed. "But… I still think we need to renegotiate our wages."

Ava wiped the sweat from her brow with her forearm, thankful she'd worn streak-free makeup.

The sun had given its performance and was now slowly making its way offstage. Across the field, the opposing team, the Red Rockets, were rushing about, running drills, fielding balls.

"I think that's everything," said Carol, handing a duffel bag filled with equipment to one of the players.

"Sammi, Marla." The girls startled at the loud voice behind them. Coach Brier motioned for them to follow her. She walked hurriedly to the main parking lot, which was quickly filling with cars. "We only have a few minutes before I'm pulled in a million different directions. So if you've got questions…"

"Understood," said Carol. "We've noticed that several of the team members have yellow armbands, and the others don't. Am I correct in deducing that they are the ones with the call signs?"

"Yes. Becky, Lilly, Chloe, Meredith, Aimee, and Karsyn are the only ones with the bands."

"And I assume you and Tina have the signs as well—or are the catchers the only ones signaling the pitchers what to throw?"

"Yes and no," said Coach Brier. "Yes, Tina and I have the call signs. Chloe and Karsyn size up the batter and signal the pitcher," she explained. "Tina and I will also send in plays as well. If the pitcher disagrees, they'll shake their head and ask for another sign. At that point, we may send in another call."

"Got it," said Carol.

"Each wristband has a grid like this." Coach Brier tilted her notepad toward them, showing them a rectangle bordered in red. Within the rectangle were six large squares, and inside those squares, twenty-five small squares. The red borders surrounding the six squares had numbers; the smaller interior squares were filled with capital letters.

	01	02	03	04	05		11	12	13	14	15		21	22	23	24	25
1	SL	CH	CB	CH	CH	1	CB	FBA	SL	FBI	CB	1	SL	CB	PI	PI	SL
2	FBA	FBI	PO	CH	SL	2	FBI	FBI	CH	CH	FBA	2	FBI	PO	SL	FBA	PI
3	FBI	CH	CH	CH	FBI	3	PO	FBA	CH	CB	FBA	3	SL	PO	PO	SL	SL
4	CB	CB	CB	FBI	PO	4	SL	CH	PI	FBA	CH	4	SL	FBA	PI	CH	PI
5	PI	FBI	CH	PI	FBA	5	PI	PI	CH	FBA	SL	5	FBI	CH	CB	FBI	FBA

	31	32	33	34	35		41	42	43	44	45		51	52	53	54	55
1	SL	FBI	CH	CH	PI	1	FBI	CH	PO	PI	SL	1	CH	PO	SL	SL	FBI
2	PI	SL	PI	CH	SL	2	PI	CB	CH	PO	SL	2	FBI	SL	SL	SL	CB
3	SL	FBI	FBA	PI	PO	3	PI	FBI	PO	SL	PI	3	PO	SL	PI	FBA	FBI
4	SL	PO	CB	FBI	SL	4	FBA	FBA	PI	SL	SL	4	PO	PI	PI	PO	CB
5	FBI	SL	PI	PI	PI	5	PI	PO	CH	CH	CH	5	PI	SL	PO	CB	SL

"That looks crazy complex," said Ava.

"It's actually *very* simple," said Coach Brier. "Let's say the catcher holds up five fingers, one finger, and then two fingers. The pitcher simply looks up the code and finds the pitch that matches the call," she explained.

"And this was developed by the cryptology department at the CIA? Still not getting it," said Ava.

"Okay, so we know the call is five, one, two, correct?"

Ava and Carol both nodded their heads.

"So, you find column fifty-one, and then you count down two spaces, and that's how you get—"

"FBI," deduced Carol, looking at the grid.

"I hardly think they're needed," joked Ava. This actually got a smile out of Coach Brier.

"It means fastball, inside," explained the coach.

	01	02	03	04	05		11	12	13	14	15		21	22	23	24	25
1	SL	CH	CB	CH	CH	1	CB	FBA	SL	FBI	CB	1	SL	CB	PI	PI	SL
2	FBA	FBI	PO	CH	SL	2	FBI	FBI	CH	CH	FBA	2	FBI	PO	SL	FBA	PI
3	FBI	CH	CH	CH	FBI	3	PO	FBA	CH	CB	FBA	3	SL	PO	PO	SL	SL
4	CB	CB	CB	FBI	PO	4	SL	CH	PI	FBA	CH	4	SL	FBA	PI	CH	PI
5	PI	FBI	CH	PI	FBA	5	PI	PI	CH	FBA	SL	5	FBI	CH	CB	FBI	FBA

	31	32	33	34	35		41	42	43	44	45		51	52	53	54	55
1	SL	FBI	CH	CH	PI	1	FBI	CH	PO	PI	SL	1	CH	PO	SL	SL	FBI
2	PI	SL	PI	CH	SL	2	PI	CB	CH	PO	SL	2	FBI	SL	SL	SL	CB
3	SL	FBI	FBA	PI	PO	3	PI	FBI	PO	SL	PI	3	PO	SL	PI	FBA	FBI
4	SL	PO	CB	FBI	SL	4	FBA	FBA	PI	SL	SL	4	PO	PI	PI	PO	CB
5	FBI	SL	PI	PI	PI	5	PI	PO	CH	CH	CH	5	PI	SL	PO	CB	SL

"But I see the letters FBI listed in a lot of boxes," said Ava.

"Yes, that's so the other team doesn't pick up on the signs. If we repeated 5-1-2 over and over, the other team would quickly figure out we're about to throw a *fastball inside*. They keep track of every call."

"So, the catcher could sign a 3-2-3," said Carol, working through the process aloud, "and that would be the same pitch."

"You've got it." Coach Brier smiled. "And, you can *bet* that the coaches on the other team are writing down the signs and trying to figure them out as the game progresses."

"Alright, so this narrows our list of suspects down to seven players," said Carol. "If someone is helping the other team, it's going to be one of the girls with the armbands."

"And," added Coach Brier, "the girls have been told *explicitly* not to share them with their teammates."

"I bet that made them popular with their friends," said Carol.

"It caused some controversy," Coach Brier agreed, "but *everything* is riding on this game. It's go big or go home. And I *don't* plan on going home empty-handed."

"Have you already given them the new calls?" asked Carol.

"No, Tina and I discussed this. We want to give the players as *little* opportunity as possible to get the signs to the other team. So we're waiting until the last minute." She looked at the girls wearily. "I know you think I'm going overboard but—"

"No, not at all," Carol insisted. "You've gotta do what you've gotta do to keep the codes safe."

"Going to be difficult to monitor," said Ava. "A simple trip to the bathroom with your phone, snap a picture, and the other team has all of your signs."

"There is a strict rule prohibiting cell phones for that very reason. They're locked up before the game. If they're caught with a phone, they're ejected from the game."

"Understandable," said Carol. "They take cheating very seriously, especially with scholarships on the line."

"At this level, yes. They used to feed cheaters to the lions in Roman times," said Coach Brier, displaying a rare hint of humor. "They've chilled quite a bit—however, it's rumored they may return to the past if cheating continues."

"I'm all for that. I'm a big fan of lions and Colosseums," said Ava. "I'll have my toga sent to the dry cleaners, just in case." She grinned.

Coach Brier chuckled and glanced at her watch. "I'm going to call a team meeting in ten minutes. I'll pass out the new call sheets to the players, while Tina meets with the other girls. From that point on"—she gave them a serious stare—"it's going to be up to you to keep an eye on things."

"We won't let you down," Carol promised.

Coach Brier nodded her thanks and, without another word, turned and made her way back toward the dugout.

"I hope that she's wrong about the cheating," said Ava.

"Me too," Carol agreed. "But if there is…"

"We feed them to the lions," Ava said dramatically.

"Exactly." Carol laughed.

CHAPTER 7
THE HAND-OFF

Like the yolk of an over-easy egg, a sliver of the sun clung to the horizon. Below, the energy in the sold-out stadium was electric. The crowd stomped their feet and clapped their hands to Queen's heart-pounding rock anthem—*We Will Rock You.*

Ava and Carol couldn't help but get caught up in the excitement.

Red Rocket fans waved handmade signs and sported glittery red rockets on their cheeks. Soul Crusher fans were decked out in bright yellow, looking like a massive cluster of bananas. If Dole wasn't a sponsor, they were missing a huge opportunity.

Carol's watch vibrated; it was a message from Derik.

Section B, row 12. Yellow baseball cap. Dead Center.

"Derik's here," said Carol. She and Ava scanned the crowd, looking for him in the sea of yellow.

It took a good thirty seconds before Ava spotted him. "There he is. Beside a shirtless man—painted yellow."

As if on cue, the man launched to his feet, raising a fist into the air, the letters *SC* emblazoned in gold on his belly.

"Eesh, my eyes," Carol groaned. "You can't unsee that."

"Derik's one lucky guy." Ava laughed.

We see you, Carol texted him.

Seconds later, a thumbs-up appeared on her screen.

Out on the field, Coach Brier and Tina were leading the girls through their pregame warm-up routine. Becky, the pitcher, warmed up with Chloe, the catcher.

"Becky is incredible," said Ava admiringly.

Carol nodded as Becky lunged forward, whipping her arm in a circle, then snapped her wrist and released a massive 14-inch ball. It rocketed through the air, terminating with a crisp smack as it hit Chloe's glove.

"That ball is huge," said Ava. "I could probably hit that thing. Looks like a globe."

"It's a warm-up ball," Carol explained. "It's supposed to make the regular ball feel easier to throw and to improve their spin."

"Oh…" Ava nodded. "Like when the boxers put on those massive gloves and then fight with the smaller ones."

"I think so." Carol nodded back.

Becky fired off several more pitches and then picked up a normal-sized softball.

With insane precision, she fired off a fastball. *Smack!*

"Seventy-seven," called out Tina, holding a device that looked like a hairdryer.

It took Ava a moment to realize Tina was talking about the speed of Becky's pitch. *Was that fast? It sure seemed fast.*

Twenty feet away, Meredith, Lilly, Aimee, and Karsyn had formed a loose square and were warming up with throws and glove work.

Carol watched as Karsyn broke from the group and jogged toward the dugout. The group converged into a triangle and continued practicing. If they thought it was unusual that Karsyn had left, they didn't show it.

Probably has to use the restroom, Carol reasoned. "Aves, I'm going to check on Karsyn; I'll be right back."

"Got it," said Ava, keeping an eye on the players.

Carol hurried across the field. She'd just made it to the dugout when she noticed Karsyn hurrying across the fence line toward a man standing at the gate, dressed in a yellow baseball hat, sunglasses, and jeans. *Weird he's wearing sunglasses at night.* He spoke to Karsyn briefly, then slipped her something black and rectangular.

Carol's watch buzzed—a text message from Derik lit up the screen.

Are you seeing this?

Yeah, Karsyn's up to something, Carol texted back.

Karsyn slid the object into her pocket, talked for another moment to the mysterious man, and then walked back along the fence line into the dugout.

Did that guy just hand her a phone? Carol followed at a distance, doing her best not to look too conspicuous.

Karsyn stood at the railing of the dugout, watching her teammates for a moment. Then she knelt and slid a duffel bag from beneath a bench.

Carol couldn't see exactly what she was doing, but she heard the *zip* of the zipper and could see Karsyn crouched down—she looked to be rummaging through her bag. A few moments later, Carol heard the *zip* again.

Karsyn stood, looked out at the field again, then walked to the back of the dugout, exiting through a door in the back that led to the locker room.

Carol took a quick look around; Ava was nowhere to be found, so she texted Derik.

I'm going to follow her.

Carol had just grabbed the door handle when she felt a hand on her shoulder, startling her, and then a girl's voice.

"Sammi? I mean—Marla?"

Carol slowly turned and exhaled, giving the girl a smile. She noticed the girl had neon yellow fingernail polish that matched her uniform.

"I didn't mean to frighten you," the girl apologized. "And… I'm horrible with names."

"It's Sammi; you got it right the first time." Carol grinned.

"I'm Blakely." The girl gave her a quick smile. "Sammi is short for Samantha, right?"

"Exactly," said Carol. "You nailed it."

"Cool." Blakely nodded. "Coach said if we needed anything, we should ask you."

"That's why I'm here," said Carol, "anything you need."

"Awesome," said Blakely. "You see that mountain of ice bags over there?"

Carol followed Blakely's gaze. She wasn't kidding; it was literally a mountain of ice.

"We need you to crush 'em up and pour them into the coolers," Blakely continued. "Stock them with drinks, then put two coolers at each end of the dugout."

"Got it!" Carol smiled, giving her a thumbs-up. *Worse timing ever.*

"Thanks. Marla is bringing over the drinks." Blakely patted Carol's shoulder, turned, and jogged back toward the field.

Carol hustled over to the tower of ice, grabbed a bag, raised it chest-high, and slammed it to the ground. Horrible timing; *Karsyn could literally be texting the other team right now*. She anxiously eyed the door to the dugout as she poured the crushed ice into the cooler.

Carol quickly looked around. No one was watching her—the ice would have to wait. She was about to slip away when Ava appeared, pushing a hand truck stacked high with cases of Gatorade and water bottles.

"Thank God!"

Ava wiped her forehead with her sleeve and sighed. "You don't know how tired I'm getting of people saying that when I show up." She glanced at Carol. "You look anxious; you didn't eat tofu again, did you?"

"What? No! Listen, a guy passed Karysn something… it looked like a phone," Carol said quietly.

"A phone?" Ava's voice took on a serious tone. "Should we tell the coach?"

"Not yet." Carol shook her head. "Not until we're certain what she's doing."

"Alright, well, where is she?"

"Girls' locker room," said Carol. "She's been in there for a while."

Ava eyed the mountain of ice. "You're obviously busy. I'll go check it out."

"But…"

Ava left Carol holding a bag of ice as she hurried into the dugout. She passed rows of benches before stopping at a rust-colored metal door set into a cinderblock wall that reminded her more of a crypt than the entrance to a locker room.

She grabbed the metal handle, pausing in the doorway. Karsyn wasn't alone. Angry voices filled the small room. Slowly, she slipped across the room to a bank of lockers and peered around the corner. The two girls were less than ten feet away, facing one another.

"I don't care, Aimee," said Karsyn angrily. "It's what the coach wants."

"Well, it makes us look bad," Aimee retorted. "The rest of the teammates feel like they can't be trusted."

"Coach is just trying to be careful," Karsyn countered. "This game is a big deal."

"*Careful*? More like paranoid," Aimee insisted.

"Coach's request seems perfectly reasonable to me." Karsyn shrugged. "Maybe you're the one who's paranoid."

A gust of wind swept through the locker room. The door flung open, then slammed shut with a violent *bang!*

Aimee whirled around, spotting Ava before she could slip back into her hiding space.

"Can we *help* you?" Aimee's eyes narrowed, her voice laced with venom.

"Hi." Ava grimaced. "I wasn't eavesdropping. I was just looking for the restroom. One Gatorade too many."

"Over there." Karsyn jerked her head toward the back of the locker room.

"Thank you!" Ava could feel their stares like knives in her back as she hurried toward the bathroom.

She sat down and quickly fired off a message to Carol.

Aimee and Karsyn arguing.

Quiet as a mouse, she listened for anything else they might say, but the girls had finished their discussion. After a moment, Ava flushed the toilet with her foot and hurried out of the bathroom. She rejoined Carol, who was dragging a large cooler across the dugout. The entire team and coaches were huddled in a tight circle, with their arms wrapped around each other.

Ava eyed the players and turned to Carol. "Someone lose a contact lens?" she joked.

"They're about to take the field for their pregame warm-up," said Carol. "This is our only chance to search Karsyn's bag."

"Keep an eye out for me," said Ava. "I'm gonna check out Karsyn's duffel bag."

CHAPTER 8
CAUGHT

Ava dropped to her hands and knees and crawled the length of the dugout to where Karsyn had stuffed her duffel bag beneath the metal bench. A cheap padlock looped through two metal hasps secured the bag. She removed a bobby pin from her hair and, seconds later, sprang the lock.

Quickly, she unzipped the bag and began rummaging through the contents. Power bars. Socks. Deodorant. More socks. But the one thing that was missing was a phone. She checked the front and side pockets—she couldn't find anything that matched Carol's description.

Ava looked up, caught Carol's eye, and shook her head, mouthing the word *nothing*.

A disappointed frown crossed Carol's face, and she motioned Ava to join her.

Ava tugged at the zipper with a little too much gusto, causing it to jam. *Oh great.* She yanked and pulled, wiggling the zipper back and forth, but it wouldn't budge. She looked up at Carol, panic flashing in her eyes.

Carol stole a quick glance over her shoulder. Van Halen's "Jump" was ending—the team was high-fiving. It looked like things were wrapping up. Carol gestured urgently for Ava to hurry.

Ava gave the zipper a final tug, but it was too late.

The coaches and players raised their hands, wiggling their fingers as they shouted, "Soul Crushers!" The word *soul* stretched out for nearly ten seconds. Then, as one, they jogged toward the dugout.

Panic surged through Ava. She dropped to the cement and rolled beneath the benches, scrambling to the back of the dugout. Commando-crawling the last few feet, she reached a stack of coolers against the far wall and slowly pushed herself to her feet.

The players poured into the dugout, excited and energized. Across the stadium, the Red Rockets took the field to the Bee Gees' hit "Stayin' Alive."

Karsyn returned to her seat and slid her bag from beneath the bench.

Ava exhaled. *Please let her think she left it open.*

Karsyn stared at her duffel bag for what felt like an eternity—and then for the second time lined up Ava in her crosshairs.

Ava could feel Karsyn's eyes stabbing her in the back while she pretended to fiddle with the coolers. *This isn't good.* She carried an empty cooler over to Carol, who was still slamming ice bags onto the ground as if she was competing in a CrossFit competition.

"She knows," Ava whispered to Carol.

"I know," Carol said quietly. "Just play it cool. She didn't *actually* catch you."

Ava nodded, but she couldn't shake the feeling that at any moment Karsyn was going to be standing right behind her.

Thankfully, that never happened.

Ava was saved when the announcer's voice boomed across the stadium.

"Singing the national anthem tonight, Miss April Jones."

A beautiful Black woman dressed in a light blue dress appeared on the massive stadium screens. The audience rose to its feet, and the players removed their hats, holding them over their hearts as Miss Jones belted out "The Star-Spangled Banner."

Ava and Carol sang along—though Ava was uncomfortably aware of the suspicious glances from Karsyn.

The song ended to thunderous applause.

As Miss Jones left the field, the announcer's voice rang out. "Play ball!"

The game was about to start. The girls were no closer to solving the mystery—and now, they really had to be on their toes. They were in Karsyn's crosshairs.

CHAPTER 9
PLAY BALL

True to her name, the Red Rockets' new pitcher, Charlie Hightower, was tall and lanky. Her age? Questionable. Standing atop the pitching rubber, she looked like King Kong, about to swat down a few planes. When she pitched, her arm spun like a nuclear-powered pinwheel. Her practice pitches scorched across the plate like a rocket.

The Soul Crushers' Kelly Stone was the first up to bat, with Aimee Martin on deck. In the field, the Red Rockets' players shifted from side to side, ready to get things going, filled with nervous energy.

Kelly settled in. She lined up her shoulders, sat into her stance, knees loose, preparing to drive through with her hips as she'd done a thousand times before.

Charlie tilted her head, her hazel eyes zeroing in on the batter. She whipped her arm in a circle and lunged forward. The softball spun across the inside of the plate—a white blur just above Kelly's knees.

"Strike!" shouted the umpire.

Ava and Carol found themselves mesmerized. It was like the epic battle between David and Goliath.

Kelly took a step back from the plate, sucked in a deep breath, tapped the bat on the ground a couple of times, and returned to the plate. She had just settled in when the pitcher threw a curveball across the plate. At first, it looked like it was going to be way outside the strike zone, but at the last moment, it curved inward, crossing the outer edge of the plate.

"Strike!"

The crowd went wild.

Charlie removed her cap, revealing a mane of red hair. She wiped her forearm across her forehead, reseated her cap, and stared down Kelly.

Kelly stepped back from the plate, focusing, attempting to shut out the roar of the crowd. She had been here before—two strikes, no balls. She just needed to settle down.

You've got this. She's not much faster than Becky, and you've been practicing with her brother Joel—and he can pitch in the 90s.

Charlie flashed Kelly a wicked smile, and that's all it took. She whipped a low inside fastball toward the plate. Kelly drove her back leg, timed her swing, and came up beneath the ball, sending it rocketing deep into right field.

The crowd jumped to their feet as Kelly rounded first base and slid into second. The Soul Crushers' dugout went crazy. The game was on!

Aimee was next up to bat.

Hightower narrowed her eyes and spat. She set her jaw and, in a whirlwind of motion, whipped her arm in a circle, snapped her wrist, and fired a fastball across the plate. The ball smacked into the catcher's glove with a loud pop.

Ava nudged Carol's shoulder. "That pitcher is scary."

"No kidding," Carol agreed. "I thought the ball was going to burst into flames."

Unrattled, Aimee returned to the plate. She settled into her stance, relaxing her mind—relying on her years of training to kick in.

The next ball flew high and to the outside. The count was one to one.

Hightower threw a changeup.

Aimee edged forward, swung and smacked the ball up the third baseline.

The Rockets' third baseman dove for the ball, rolled, leapt to her feet—and overthrew first. A costly error.

"Go! Go! Go!" Tina yelled, waving her arms for Kelly to take home.

The Rockets player fired the ball toward home plate. The catcher sprinted forward, scooped it up and charged the plate—but it was too late. Kelly scored, and Aimee slid safely into third.

The Soul Crushers were on their feet, celebrating, high-fiving Kelly as she jogged back to the dugout.

The Red Rockets' catcher called a timeout and walked toward the pitcher's mound. Hightower sneered at her and shooed her away. A loud collective gasp filled the stadium.

Meredith was up next. She was one of the Soul Crushers' strongest batters. If Hightower thought things were going to get better, she was sorely mistaken. Meredith held the league record for home runs.

"She'll probably walk her," said Carol.

"I don't know," said Ava. "I think the pitcher has too much pride."

"Like it's—"

A mighty crack filled the air as Meredith smacked Hightower's first pitch over the fence for a home run. It was more than the Soul Crushers could take. They rushed the field, high-fiving Aimee and Meredith as they crossed home plate.

The crowd was on its feet, stomping and shouting, "Soul Crushers! Soul Crushers!"

This time the Red Rockets coach charged the mound. The scowl on her face showed that this clearly wasn't the result she expected from their new pitcher.

The score was 3-0. Half the audience was cheering, the other half, shell-shocked by the one-sided game.

In an unexpected move, the coach pulled Hightower and brought in seasoned pitcher, Roberta Gonzales, who had been warming up on the sidelines.

The umpire allowed her a few warm-up pitches. "Last one," he called, then restarted the game.

Roberta was an exceptionally skilled pitcher and managed to hold the Soul Crushers at three runs.

Lilly pitched the next inning and held the Rockets to one run.

By the end of the fourth inning, the Soul Crushers were up by three runs.

"Five more innings," said Ava excitedly. "If they can keep this up, everything is going to be fine."

"Still," Carol cautioned, "we need to keep our eyes open."

The words had barely left Carol's mouth when the crowd leapt to their feet. Only it wasn't the Soul Crushers jumping up and down—it was the Red Rockets. Hightower had just smashed the ball out of the stadium. She drove two of her teammates home, making the score 4 to 4, a tie game.

CHAPTER 10
BASES LOADED

The atmosphere in the stadium was electric. The Soul Crushers had fought back tooth and nail and secured a one-run lead. There were two outs, the bases were loaded, and Kara, a.k.a. Mini Hulk, approached the plate.

Hightower was back on the mound. She shot Kara a scathing look and curled her lips into an evil smile.

"Oh, she's got your number," the catcher mocked Kara.

With a quick, powerful lunge, Hightower threw the pitch. The ball rocketed through the air, crossing over the inside corner of the plate, low, just above Kara's knees.

She swung hard, the bat cutting through the air, missing the ball.

"Woah, maybe you need a bigger bat," laughed the catcher as she stood, throwing the ball back to Hightower.

Kara ignored the smack talk and settled in, calming her breathing. *You've got this.*

"Strike number two, coming up," the catcher taunted.

Hightower was already in motion, her arm arced powerfully, her wrist snapped as her front foot simultaneously impacted; the ball blazed across the plate like an asteroid.

"Strike!" yelled the umpire.

Kara stepped back from the plate and tapped the bat on the ground. She looked out at her teammates. They really needed a big play.

Meredith, who was currently occupying third base, knew exactly how to help. As Kara returned to the plate, Meredith, the fastest player on their team, began slowly edging toward home.

Suddenly, Hightower's attention was divided. She whirled on the mound, threw the ball to third, just as Meredith dove back to safety. She stood and dusted herself off, giving the pitcher a huge grin.

As soon as Hightower set up again, Meredith began shuffling along the baseline. Hightower whipped the ball to third, but Meredith dove back, beating the throw.

A scowl crossed Hightower's face. Meredith was toying with her, trying to break her rhythm. She took a deep breath, wound up, and threw—the ball spinning into an evil curve.

Kara cut in low, bringing the bat up at an angle, catching the underside of the ball, launching it deep into right field. Meredith crossed the plate, Lilly rounded third and slid into home a millisecond before the catcher caught it.

The score was now seven to four!

Ava jumped up and down, pumping her fist in the air. "You know what's happening?" she said, turning to Carol. "It's our presence. Our *renowned* investigative skills have deterred the other team from cheating."

"Yeah." Carol chuckled. "I'm *sure* that's what it is. Nothing to do with the players' talent… or the thousands of hours of practice they've put in."

"Nope." Ava smiled. "We generate what I like to call an *investigative aura*—feared by wrongdoers."

Carol crossed her arms and dipped her chin. "I'm going to stop you before you go full throttle into a theatrical speech."

"My Shakesperean voice has moved people to tears."

"Frightened children, shattered windows, caused a mass exodus of wildlife."

Ava sniffed. "Jealousy is *not* a good color on you."

Carol smirked. "Says the person wearing neon yellow."

"You're one to talk," said Ava.

"Speaking of people wearing neon yellow," Carol continued, her tone shifting, "we never figured out what that guy gave Karsyn."

"Are you sure he actually gave her something? Like maybe he showed her his phone and she gave it back?" Ava suggested.

"No, she definitely had something…"

"Well, it's not in her bag," said Ava, "and not on her person. You can't hide anything under these uniforms."

"It's got to be in her locker," said Carol.

"I can check." Ava casually peeked over her shoulder.

Karsyn was wiping her helmet off with a cloth. She looked up and met Ava's eyes and glared at her.

Ava slowly rotated her head back around and whispered, "I think we should wait until she goes back on the field."

"You're about to get your wish," Carol said as the stadium erupted. "Hightower just struck out Chloe."

While Coach Brier and Tina huddled with the players, Ava and Carol sprang into action. Carol busied herself restocking the coolers, and Ava grabbed a trash bag and began collecting discarded power bar wrappers and empty bottles of Gatorade strewn around the dugout.

Out on the field, Becky was warming up, throwing practice pitches with Chloe.

Ava threw the trash bag over her shoulder and entered the locker room. She left the bag by the door and quickly surveyed the room, making sure it was empty. Moments later, Carol slipped inside.

"Welcome to my humble domain," Ava said quietly.

"It's nice." Carol smiled. "I love what you've done with the lighting." She made her way over to the row of lockers, studying them. "I wonder which one is hers."

Ava pulled back her sleeve and checked her watch. Carol looked at her expectantly.

"*Third* corn dog," Ava sighed, shaking her head.

"What?" Carol asked, giving Ava a questioning look.

"Derik texted, 'Third corn dog,' and sent a barfing emoji. He's living his best life and we—"

"Not helpful," said Carol flatly. "We need to hurry."

"So, I shouldn't reply?"

"No, we need to figure out which locker is—"

"It's either this one or this one," Ava interrupted, pointing.

"And how do you know that?"

"I saw her hang her hoodie inside," said Ava. "Guard the door, and I'll check them out."

"Okay." Carol gave a quick nod, moving to the end of the lockers where she had a clear view of the door.

Ava examined the combination lock; it was the same type they had at school. A silver casing encircled a black dial marked with white numbers zero through fifty. In the center of the dial was a keyhole.

Ava lifted the bottom of her hoodie, revealing a crossbody bag strapped beneath it. She unzipped it and removed a small leather pouch containing her lock-picking tools. In less than a minute, she'd popped the first locker open.

"Empty," Ava announced quietly.

She closed the door and was just about to move onto the next locker when the dugout room door swung open with a *bang*, and Aimee stepped inside. She'd entered so quickly, Carol was caught by surprise.

"Aimee," Carol cried out, warning Ava.

Ava bolted away, having just enough of a warning to dash into the bathroom and soundlessly slip into a stall.

Aimee was clearly surprised to see Carol and made no effort to hide it.

"Emptying the trash." Carol smiled, tilting her head toward a trash can. "I'm a bit of a neat freak."

Aimee raised her eyebrows and smirked, as if to say *not interested*.

"Guess I'm back at it," said Carol, heading for the door.

Once again, Ava found herself in the bathroom, listening. A locker door clanged open, then silence.

Ava waited, counting the seconds in her head. Five… ten… fifteen. Nothing. She raised her wrist and tapped out a message to Carol.

Did she leave?

Seconds later, Ava's watch buzzed. *No.*

Ava swallowed. She shifted her weight, inching closer to the stall door. She was about to sneak out and take a peek when the locker door slammed shut. She could hear Aimee's hurried footsteps, and then the dugout door slamming closed.

Ava's watch buzzed again. *She's out.*

Ava shot a quick thumbs-up to Carol, then hurried to Karsyn's locker. Her fingers shook as adrenaline surged through her body. She slipped the lockpick kit out of her hoodie and grabbed the torque wrench and the pick. It took a matter of seconds when—*click*. She was in.

Ava swung the door open. It was empty except for a white hoodie that hung from a hook at the back of the locker. She cast a quick look over her shoulder and slipped her hand inside the front pocket.

"Gotcha," Ava whispered. Only the black rectangular object she held in her hand wasn't a phone; it was a thin cardboard box.

She quickly opened it, revealing a black felt lining with a thin circular indentation—suggesting it had either contained a necklace or a bracelet. A folded piece of paper lay snug against one end. Ava knew she shouldn't look, but she had to know.

It was a handwritten letter.

I love you so much. Mom would have been so proud! Love, Dad.

Ava's face blossomed red with shame. She slowly closed the box and returned it to Karsyn's hoodie. *No wonder Karsyn's been on edge.*

She closed the locker and headed toward the door.

CHAPTER 11
THE ROCKETS SURGE

Like the eye of a cyclops, a full moon rose above the stadium, unblinking, watching the game. A digital rocket flashed across the scoreboard, exploding into thousands of pixels as the Red Rockets jogged onto the field. It was the bottom of the sixth, and they were down by three. Things were looking good for the Soul Crushers.

Becky took to the pitcher's mound and fired off several practice throws. Feeling confident, she nodded to Chloe, the catcher. She tossed the ball back and dropped into a crouch.

"Time in!" yelled the umpire.

As the Red Rocket player entered the batter's box, Chloe flashed one-four-three with her fingers.

Becky nodded, waiting for the Red Rocket player to settle in.

The girl at bat adjusted her helmet, settled in, staring down Becky.

Becky rolled the ball around in her glove, waiting until it felt just right in her hand. She angled off, whipped her arm, snapped her wrist, and released the ball. It sailed through the air, breaking off into a curve as it approached the plate.

The Red Rocket player adjusted effortlessly, her bat making contact with the ball, sending it deep into centerfield.

Becky spun, watching her teammates sprint toward the ball as the player rounded first base and headed for second.

Kelly threw the ball to Meredith on third, holding the Red Rocket player at second.

Becky circled the pitcher's mound for a moment. This wasn't how she wanted the inning to begin. She took a deep breath, nodded, and smacked the ball against her glove. She recognized the next girl, Trixy Zelaya. She was a solid hitter and fast as lightning. Her weakness: the fastball.

Trixy knocked her bat against her cleats, rolled her shoulders, and stepped up to the plate.

Becky glanced in for the sign.

Chloe flashed one-five-four—changeup.

Becky thought for a beat, then gave a subtle shake of her head.

Behind the plate, Chloe reset, cycling through the signs before settling on a new call.

In the batter's box, Trixy stiffened. She took a step back, tapping her bat against her cleats once again. She adjusted her helmet, re-centered herself, and focused on Becky.

The next pitch screamed across the plate and was met with a meaty *smack*. The ball shot off like a bullet, hugging the chalk line down third. It stayed low, just a screaming blur skipping inches above the dirt.

Meredith barely had time to react. Instinctively, she flicked out her glove, but it was too late; the ball had already zipped past her. A streak of white kicked up a spray of infield dust as it rocketed into shallow left.

It was a nightmare play as a Red Rocket player scored, and another slid into third.

The crowd was on their feet, cheering, yelling along with the organ.

Dun. Dun. Dun. Dun. Charge!

Carol's watch buzzed. She glanced at the screen, a message from Coach Brier.

Keep your eyes open.

"Who is it?" asked Ava.

"Coach Brier." Carol quickly texted Derik.

Seconds later, Derik replied, *On it.*

The Soul Crushers lined the dugout railing, yelling out encouragement to Becky. If she heard them, it wasn't apparent. She stood behind the circle, glove pressed to her hip. The Red Rockets had rallied with two solid hits, back to back. Both scorched.

Becky exhaled, took a deep breath, and exhaled again. She looked up into the audience; Melinda Morgan, dressed in a burnt-orange polo, holding a radar gun, sat facing her, directly behind home plate. She was a well-known scout from the University of Oklahoma—home of the legendary Oklahoma Sooners Softball team. *No pressure.*

Becky nodded at the signal, wound up, and threw.

It was like déjà vu; the Red Rocket player bunted the ball.

Becky hustled, racing the player dashing from third toward home. She scooped up the ball and tossed it to Chloe, holding the runner at third. Becky had stopped the Red Rockets from scoring.

Hightower stalked up to the plate, oozing confidence, bat resting across her shoulder like a club. She dug the toe of her cleat into the dirt of the batter's box and took a slow practice swing.

Becky eyed the powerful hitter. She'd struck her out twice already; she'd do it again. She flexed her fingers inside the glove and gave herself a small nod.

Behind the plate, Chloe flashed the sign—fastball, inside.

Hightower stepped out of the box for a moment, tugged at her batting glove, then pulled the brim of her helmet low. She stepped back in and settled into her stance, bat cocked high over her shoulder. She looked like a warrior about to strike.

A millisecond after Becky's arm rotated forward, Hightower shifted back from the plate, giving herself room space to swing. The bat blurred through the strike zone—and the thunderous *CRACK* of the bat echoed off the walls of the stadium.

Becky's head snapped toward left field.

The ball cleared the fence, disappearing into the night as the crowd erupted.

Becky stood frozen on the mound, glove hanging by her side. It was like a horrible dream.

Hightower raised her arm and waved to the crowd as she rounded the bases. Her teammates poured from the dugout, shouting, hugging her, and slapping high-fives along the third baseline. The score was 7 to 8; the Red Rockets had taken the lead.

"Time!" shouted Coach Brier.

"Time," echoed the plate umpire, both arms raised.

Coach Brier hustled to the mound. Chloe and the infielders drifted in to join her.

"Did you see Hightower shift back before the pitch was even thrown?" asked Carol.

"Yeah." Ava nodded. "The coach is right. They're definitely signaling the batters."

"It could be coming from their dugout," Carol suggested.

Ava looked across the field toward the Red Rockets' dugout. "I don't think so. They'd have to have a clear view of Chloe's hand signals—and," she added, "they'd have to crack the code and let the batter know what pitch is coming."

"It's a lot," Carol agreed. "But we've got to start somewhere."

"Remember what you said about treating the clues like a math problem?" said Ava. "I think we can figure out who is stealing the signals and make it so only a few people can see Chloe's signal."

"Awesome!" encouraged Carol.

"So, here's what's bouncing around in my *caballo*," Ava said, tapping her head with a finger.

"*Caballo* is horse," Carol sighed. "I think you mean *cabeza*."

"Probably," Ava agreed. "Right now, a *lot* of people can see Chloe's hands when she gives the signal. We need to limit the amount of people that can see her signals."

"How?"

"Easy, we have her shift her leg, and cover the signal with her hand, so it's difficult for anyone but the pitcher to see it."

"That's good." Carol nodded. "That makes sense."

"And, to find out who is stealing the call sheets and giving them to the Red Rockets, we have the players switch out their call bands right before the other team goes up to bat."

"The person would be forced to send the new band information to the person signaling the batters," said Carol.

"Yep." Ava nodded. "And the good thing is, we'll only have to keep our eye on the six players with the bands."

"So for now, we tell Coach Brier to have Chloe hide the calls and, in the next inning, switch out the bands."

"I know it's not perfect," said Ava, "but for now, it's our best option."

Carol glanced out at the field. The players were returning to their positions. "We need to talk to Coach Brier—asap."

CHAPTER 12
COVERT SIGNALS

Ava's plan worked.

Becky struck out the next two players back to back. The third batter managed only a weak base hit and the final batter popped the ball into shallow centerfield where it was easily caught, ending the seventh inning.

As the Soul Crushers jogged off the field, they praised Becky as they headed toward the dugout. She smiled and high-fived her teammates, but the truth was, she was rattled—her future was riding on this game.

The girls huddled around Coach Brier, listening and nodding as she quickly discussed their game plan for the next inning. The score was eight to seven in favor of the Red Rockets.

The crowd cheered as the Red Rockets jogged back onto the field.

"At least they can't cheat right now," said Ava.

Carol gave a quick nod. "Let's just hope they score."

Hightower fired a series of warm-up throws to the catcher, each one terminating with a sharp *pop* as it smacked into the glove. She turned and spat over her shoulder as Karsyn stepped into the batter's box.

Ava watched Karsyn, emotions tugging at her heart. She swallowed back the guilt she felt for invading something so private. When this was all over, she would apologize. Her heartbeat fired off like a machine gun just thinking about it.

Karsyn tugged at her bright yellow jersey, swung the bat a couple times, then turned her head toward the stands.

Ava followed her gaze, recognizing the man in the audience—baseball cap, sunglasses. The mysterious man who had given her the black box was her father. He smiled at Karsyn and tapped his heart twice with his fingertips.

Karsyn returned the gesture, then turned back to face Hightower—her face said *bring it on.*

Ava closed her eyes, whispering a quick prayer, willing Karsyn to hit the ball.

Seconds later, there was a sharp *crack*, followed by the roar of the crowd. The words *HOME RUN!* flashed across the scoreboard. With one swing of the bat, Karsyn had tied the game!

Eight to eight.

Ava pumped her fist in the air. "Thank you," she whispered over the screaming from the dugout.

Over the next fifteen gut-wrenching minutes, the Soul Crushers battled back. Hightower deliberately began walking the best hitters. When she did challenge the batters, she threw high-speed, dangerously close inside pitches—trying to intimidate them.

Despite the Red Rockets' best efforts, the Soul Crushers clawed their way back and were able to expand their lead to a one-point game.

Carol's watch buzzed as the players jogged in from the field. She pulled back her sleeve to check the message on her watch. It was from Derik.

BRB restroom.

Not yet, Carol replied. *Coach is about to switch bands.*

Two large sodas, four corn dogs, Derik replied, ending with a vomit emoji.

Hang on five minutes.

Ugh! If you hear a loud pop, it's me.

Least you'll go out with a bang.

Not funny.

"Everything okay?" asked Ava, sidling up beside her.

"Derik needs the restroom." Carol grinned. "He's attempting to eat his weight in corn dogs."

Ava arched her eyebrows. "TMI."

"Keep your eyes open," said Carol, her voice turning serious. "Coach is about to switch out the bands."

"Alright, bring it in!" Coach Brier called, clapping her hands.

The team gathered in a tight semicircle inside the dugout, slipping off their helmets, tucking their gloves under their arms.

Coach Brier scanned their faces. "We're doing great, guys," she said firmly. "Good energy that last inning. Let's keep the pressure on. We've got this."

The girls nodded in unison.

Coach Brier lowered her voice slightly. "We're switching up the call bands once more."

A few of the girls exchanged quick looks.

Lilly spoke first. "Do you think they're cheating?"

"Let's just say we're keeping a close eye on things."

"You seriously think they would cheat?" Karsyn asked.

"Maybe," Coach Brier said calmly. "Maybe not. But we're not giving them the chance."

"They would instantly forfeit the game," said Karsyn.

"The Houston Astros cheated in the World Series in 2017," Coach Brier replied. "When the stakes are high, people become desperate."

"That's crazy," said Lilly, more to herself than anyone else.

Tina stepped forward and motioned to the girls wearing bands. She collected the old inserts and handed out fresh call sheets, watching carefully as each girl slid them into place.

"Alright, we've got about a minute," said Coach Brier. "Do what you've gotta do, and then let's lock it down this inning."

Ava and Carol busied themselves as the group split up. Several girls hurried into the locker room, while others broke off alone or in small clusters, taking bites of power bars and fresh fruit and washing it all down with long pulls from their sports drinks.

Carol grabbed a trash bag and casually fell in behind Lilly and Aimee—both wearing their call bands—as they headed into the locker room.

The girls queued up in front of the bathroom stalls. Carol hung back, trying not to be too conspicuous, as she kept a watchful eye on Lilly and Aimee at the end of the line. She quickly let her eyes rove over their uniforms, looking for the telltale outline of a phone tucked beneath the fabric. Nothing.

Aimee shot a quick look over her shoulder, her eyes meeting Carol's. Something in her look—cool, deliberate—sent a prickle crawling up the back of Carol's neck. *Did Karsyn say something to her?* Carol dropped to one knee beside a bench and scooped up a crumpled power bar wrapper, stuffing it into the trash bag. When she straightened, Aimee was still watching. Carol offered a friendly smile and turned away, moving a little faster than she meant to.

Back in the dugout, Ava kept a close eye on Becky, Chloe, Karsyn, and Meredith. Karsyn suddenly looked up and caught Ava staring. She held her gaze for a beat, then made a slow, deliberate show of zipping her duffel bag shut, slipping a padlock through two metal rings and securing it.

Ava could feel her face burning; she was sure it was bright red. She turned away quickly and dropped to one knee beside the cooler near the gate leading to the field. Lifting the lid, she leaned over it, using the motion as a cover.

Under the pretense of restocking, she tapped out a quick message on her watch.

Help keep an eye out on the dugout. Karsyn is suspicious.

His reply came almost instantly—a pair of eyes.

Ava exhaled and reached for a twenty-four-pack of water, tearing open the plastic wrap and dropping bottles in one by one. Out of the corner of her eye, she caught Becky and Chloe walking past, heading toward Coach Brier and Tina.

Ava shut the cooler lid and stood.

Karsyn slammed into Ava's shoulder, nearly knocking her against the cooler as she passed by with Meredith.

"Uncool," said Ava under her breath.

Meredith glanced back once… then quickly looked away.

Woah, I saw that, Derik texted.

She officially hates me, Ava replied.

Why?

Will fill you in later.

Carol knotted the trash bag and dropped it into a can near the door. Then she crossed the room to the row of sinks along the wall.

The locker room had gone quiet.

Lilly and Aimee must still be in the stalls. Carol turned the faucet. Cold water rushed over her hands, loud in the silence. She grabbed a paper towel from the dispenser, dried her hands quickly, and slipped away, ducking behind a row of lockers just as the toilets began to flush and stall doors banged open.

Water hissed from the sinks as the girls stepped out.

Through the noise, Carol could hear Lilly and Aimee talking… and then the sound of footsteps drawing closer.

"You go ahead," said Aimee. "I'll be right there."

Carol pressed herself flat and peered around the edge of the lockers.

Aimee stood, facing the other set of lockers. She stole a quick glance over her shoulder. Then moved quickly to the center bench and knelt, her back to Carol. Her hands were doing something, but Carol couldn't see what.

Carol shifted her weight, edging toward the far end of the row for a better angle, when the door flew open, slamming against the wall.

Carol lurched sideways. Her knee drove hard into the metal locker with a hollow *bang*. She scrambled backward, pressing herself against the wall, and looked up into the shadow looming over her.

"What are you doing?" asked Kelly.

A second later, Aimee bolted around the corner and stopped short.

"I dropped my earring," said Carol, her voice steadier than she felt. She uncurled her fingers to reveal a small gold loop resting in her palm. "It rolled behind the locker. Sorry." She gave an embarrassed smile. "I didn't mean to startle anyone."

"Startle?" Aimee's face grew dark. "You were snooping," she hissed.

"What?" Carol gasped. "No!" She was surprised by the venom in Aimee's voice.

"Come on," insisted Kelly, resting a hand on Aimee's shoulder. "Coach sent me to get you."

Aimee held Carol's gaze for one long moment. She spun on her heel and followed Kelly out the door.

The door swung shut with a dull thud.

Carol sat on the cold cement floor, her heart pounding. She rubbed her knee and pushed herself up, her hands trembling slightly.

Aimee had just moved to the top of their suspect list.

CHAPTER 13
OPERATION LOCKER ROOM

Becky and Chloe talked for a moment, fist-bumped, then jogged to their positions. Becky turned the ball slowly in her hand, inspecting the seams, then settled into her stance and began her warm-up pitches—clean, crisp, precise. There was something deeply satisfying about the sharp *smack* of the ball snapping into the catcher's mitt.

"I'm telling you, she was acting suspicious," said Carol. "And the way she looked at me…"

"It was like *magic*," Ava teased.

"Seriously."

"Maybe Karsyn said something to her?"

Carol mulled it over, her face said *maybe*.

"She shoulder-checked me on the way to the field," Ava revealed. "She's officially marked me for death."

"That's mature." Carol frowned. "No—I think Aimee hid something under one of the benches. I just couldn't check with them watching me."

The stadium pipe organ burst to life, startling the girls.

Behind home plate, the umpire raised his arm and bellowed, "Play ball!"

The first Red Rocket player stepped into the batter's box, tapping her cleats with the bat before settling it across her shoulder. Along the dugout rail, the Soul Crushers leaned forward in a row, clapping and shouting encouragement to their teammates.

Ava nudged Carol's shoulder and tilted her head toward the locker room. "Come on," she whispered. "While everyone's distracted."

They moved one at a time, drifting toward the back of the dugout, careful to look casual. When no one was watching, they slipped through the door. Inside, a fluorescent light flickered overhead, buzzing like a mosquito. Otherwise, the locker room was eerily quiet.

"Aimee was kneeling right here," said Carol, crossing to the center bench.

She dropped to her knees and pressed her cheek close to the floor, peering beneath the wooden bench. There, taped against the underside was a small black pouch secured with a strip of silver duct tape.

Carol pulled up the hem of her hoodie, unzipped her crossbody bag, and removed a pair of latex gloves. She quickly snapped them on and peeled the tape back. She reached inside the pouch and slid out a thin black phone.

"Bingo," said Carol softly.

"Is that a phone?" Ava asked, her eyes darting from the device to the door and back.

"Yep." Carol pressed the button on the side. The screen lit up instantly. She swiped her finger across it and tapped the gallery icon—then froze.

"Oh man," she whispered. "Take a look at this." She turned the phone so Ava could see.

There were only three images. Each one was a crisp, close-up photograph of the Soul Crushers' call card—every sign, every signal.

"What do we do?" asked Ava, her voice barely above a whisper, her eyes still darting from the phone to the door.

"I'll send the pictures to myself," said Carol. "That way we have the evidence—and the number tied to this phone."

"And whoever she's been sending them to," added Ava.

Carol nodded, already moving. She forwarded the images to her own phone, then quickly deleted the sent messages. She scrolled through the thread, reading to herself for a moment before looking up.

"Aimee's only been texting one person," said Carol. "Someone named Max."

"Max," Ava echoed. "I don't think we know a Max."

"Listen to this," said Carol, reading the text exchange: *One for a fastball. Two for a fastball inside. Three for a curveball. Four for a changeup.*

The words hung in the air between them.

Carol took a screenshot of the conversation, sent it to her phone, then deleted the thread. She slipped the phone back into the pouch and pressed the tape firmly into place beneath the bench.

"I can't believe it," Ava whispered.

"I know." Carol sat back on her heels. She looked up at Ava, her face caught somewhere between satisfaction and dread. "Coach Brier is going to be heartbroken."

CHAPTER 14
REVEALED

Coach Brier anxiously tapped her pen against her notepad. The Red Rockets had runners on first and third. The play would be at home—they had to stop the runner from scoring.

The batter swung late, barely catching the outside edge of the pitch and sending the ball spinning up toward the backstop. Chloe threw off her mask and scrambled beneath the ball, her eyes locked on it as it tumbled down. She dove in a cloud of dust and came up with it cradled in her glove.

Elliot Molina didn't hesitate. She tagged third and exploded toward home, her cleats chewing up the dirt in rapid-fire bursts, chalk dust spraying behind her with every stride. She was fast—dangerously fast.

But Becky had already read the play before the ball hit the backstop and was charging toward home, her arm out and waiting. Chloe spun on her knee and rocketed the ball to her. Becky caught it and spun, stretching the tag down onto Elliot's ankle just as Elliot came in hard, the collision knocking Becky flat.

For one long second, nobody breathed.

"Out!" The umpire's arm shot into the air.

The Soul Crushers dugout exploded. Girls spilled against the railing, screaming and pounding the fence as Becky climbed to her feet and pumped her fist, then reached down to offer Elliot a hand up.

Elliot swatted Becky's hand away, and stormed off.

Across the diamond, the Red Rockets coach snatched her clipboard off the bench and hurled it to the ground. She stepped onto the field and threw her arm into the air.

"Time!"

Becky brushed the dirt from her uniform as she and her teammates jogged in. It was a one-point game. Every play mattered. The girls poured out of the dugout to meet them—a blur of high-fives and fist bumps. Coach Brier moved through them, offering words of encouragement before sending the girls back out to the field.

Carol watched from the back of the dugout, chewing her lip.

"I'm going to go talk to the coach," she said.

Ava glanced at her. "Good luck."

"Believe me, I don't want to," said Carol, frowning. "But I feel I have to."

"Yeah." Ava nodded slowly, thinking.

Carol was already turning to go, when Ava caught her arm. "Tell her not to pull Aimee out of the game yet."

Carol gave her a questioning look.

"If Aimee is suddenly pulled, Max is going to know something's up." Ava's eyes drifted out to the field. "We've got to find Max first. Remember, the Red Rockets are last to bat. If they have all the call signs—"

"It could end badly," said Carol.

"Very badly." Ava nodded.

Carol exhaled. "I don't know if the coach will go along with that."

"If she wants to win the game," said Ava, "and for us to find Max, then she'll do what's best for the team."

"I'll do my best," Carol sighed.

"You've got this," Ava said encouragingly, a sly grin slipping across her face. "And look at it this way—if things go sideways, you've only shattered the hopes and dreams of a dozen or so girls." Ava smiled and spread her hands. "No pressure."

Carol shot her one last look and walked away.

CHAPTER 15
BAD TO WORSE

Coach Brier took the news about Aimee surprisingly well. It was as if she had already come to terms with the possibility that someone on her team was cheating. The only telltale sign that it affected her at all was a large, pulsing vein that appeared on her forehead.

Carol could literally tell every time Coach Brier's heart beat.

If the news about Aimee wasn't bad enough, out on the pitcher's mound, Becky was favoring her right ankle. The collision with Elliot had clearly done some damage.

"So, you know for sure Aimee sent off the new calls to the spy," said Coach Brier slowly, as if chewing the words. She glanced at Carol for a moment, then back at the field.

"Yes—she sent the photos to someone named Max."

"Any idea who this Max is?" asked Coach Brier, her eyes still on the field.

"We think Max is a spectator," said Carol, "with a direct line of sight to Chloe. Our friend Derik checked the team roster, and there's no one with a first or last name starting with Max."

"I see." Coach Brier nodded, deep in thought.

Out on the field, Chloe flashed Becky the call. Becky paused, then gave a quick shake of her head. At the plate, the Red Rocket batter stepped out of the box, rolling her shoulders and picking at her batting glove—burning time.

A moment later, Chloe sent a new call.

"Did you see that?" Carol asked. "The batter stepped back to buy herself time to get the signal. She *never* looked to the dugout or at the stadium."

Coach Brier nodded, her jaw tightening.

Carol watched the batter intently. *Somehow*, Max was sending her the call. She quickly fired off a text to Ava. *Watch Aimee—see if she is signaling the batter.*

On it, Ava texted back.

Out on the field, Becky stared down the batter, set her jaw, and with a whirl of her arm, fired a fastball toward the plate. A quick grimace flashed across her face as she lunged forward, her cleat driving into the dirt.

Before the ball had even left Becky's fingertips, the batter was already moving, shifting her weight, arcing her bat up in a perfect path beneath the pitch and sending it deep into right field. It caromed off the wall as Kelly chased it down. A Red Rocket player crossed home plate, the crowd cheering them on. The batter slid into third, standing to brush the dirt from her uniform as the Red Rockets' dugout erupted.

Carol glanced at the scoreboard, her heart sank; the Red Rockets tied the game.

The stadium organ thundered—*dun, dun, dun, dun*—and the crowd answered as one: "Charge!"

Coach Brier closed her eyes and let out a long breath. Tina appeared at her shoulder, a worried look on her face.

"Coach," said Carol, "I have a plan, but I'm going to need you to buy me a little time."

"Time?" Coach Brier croaked. "That's something we don't have."

"That's why we've got to hurry," said Carol, her voice tight with urgency. "Coach, call a timeout. Pull Becky and Chloe aside—just you three and nobody else. Tell Chloe to throw out three signals. Becky picks the *second* one. It will be too much for Max to track. It should give me enough time to find him."

"It's a tie game," said Coach Brier. "If you can't prove they're cheating…"

Her words trailed off, heavy with doubt.

"We'll figure it out," Carol said. "I *promise*."

Coach Brier studied her for a quick beat and then nodded. "Alright, I'll buy you as much time as I can."

Carol hurried away toward the dugout, unnoticed. Along the railing, the Soul Crushers stood frozen, their eyes locked on the field. They all knew they had one last chance at bat—one last chance to win the New England Nationals.

CHAPTER 16
THE HUNT BEGINS

Carol and Ava slipped into the empty locker room, pausing for a moment, listening to make sure it was empty. A moth flitted above, bumping against the fluorescent light.

"I think I've got it figured out," said Carol, walking toward the lockers.

"Why you have no friends?" Ava grinned.

"No, numbskull, how they're stealing the calls," Carol said as she hurried over to her locker, twisting the combination dial.

"Awesome," said Ava. "Enlighten me."

"I'm pretty certain it's some kind of wearable device that vibrates," said Carol. "Something tiny enough to hide without being noticeable."

Ava began spinning her combination dial, thinking. "If Max is sending a signal—"

"We can track it." Carol nodded, finishing Ava's thought.

"Like when we tracked that guy's Wi-Fi in Nantucket?"

"Similar," said Carol. She slid her backpack out of her locker and shrugged it onto her shoulder. "I'm pretty sure Max isn't using Wi-Fi. He'd be using a simple signal, like a garage door opener."

"So… you're saying, we're looking for someone clicking a garage door opener?" Ava snorted.

"I'll explain later," said Carol. "Grab your stuff."

"But you can track it, right?" Ava asked, following Carol into the bathroom.

"That's the plan."

"But we're talking about a crowd of over two thousand people."

"Aves." Carol spun, facing her. "We don't have to search the entire crowd, only the people that have a direct line of sight to Chloe's calls. That rules out two-thirds of the crowd."

Ava thought for a moment, tracing figures in the air. "Two-thirds of two thousand, carry the one—"

"Oh my gosh, get changed," groaned Carol. She ducked into a stall and slammed the door. "And text Derik—let him know we're coming. I'll work on the emergency door so we can sneak out."

Ava quickly pulled on her sweats and fired off a quick message. Seconds later, Derik replied with a thumbs-up. She slipped into her sneakers and hurried over to Carol, who was crouched beside a rusty metal door, studying the alarm system.

The words *EMERGENCY EXIT ONLY* were stenciled in red above a smaller warning: *Alarm will sound if opened.*

"Can you bypass it?" Ava asked, eyeing the snaking gray wire that ran to a small box mounted above the door.

"Mere child's play." Carol grinned. "It's a simple magnetic contact alarm—break the contact, the alarm triggers."

"Oh, like the one in Vermont," said Ava.

"Exactly." Carol unzipped the front pocket of her backpack and pulled out a brushed aluminum case no bigger than a matchbox. She flipped it open, revealing a dull silver disc nestled inside a fitted foam insert.

"Behold—the neodymium magnet, from the faraway lands of—"

"Amazon Prime," Carol intoned.

Ava gave a disappointed frown. "You really need to work more on your reveal. If it were me, it would be like *The Lion King*—I'd hold out Simba, angels singing. Or like Thor and his hammer. I beckon thee, oh mighty hammer—"

Ava held out her hand, making a *ka-chung* sound as if catching the hammer midair.

"Read the room," Carol sighed. "We don't have time to be dramatic," she said, pressing the magnet against the door.

"We're teenage girls. There's *always* time to be dramatic."

Carol stood and eased the door open a couple inches. Rust flakes and debris rained down on her.

Ava held back a snicker. "Perhaps a new dandruff shampoo?"

"Be quiet," Carol shot back. She peeked outside. Thankfully, all eyes were on the game.

Carol took a quick glance at the field—Becky was back at the plate. Their only chance to catch

Max was when she was pitching, which put the Soul Crushers in a precarious position.

"Come on," urged Carol. "Let's go!"

CHAPTER 17
BLIP

Ava, Carol, and Derik climbed deep into the stadium, working their way toward the back of the complex. No one seemed to notice or care that Carol's head was bent over her laptop—they were too busy watching the game.

A wall of neon-blue static filled Carol's screen as she watched for any unusual signals.

Far below on the field, Becky and Chloe were following the plan. Rotate through the signs rapidly to confuse Max. So far, it seemed to be working.

"Here," Derik said, pointing to an empty stretch of bench where Carol could sit and work on her laptop.

"Got anything, Big Brain?" Ava asked, scanning the sea of people.

"Any second now," Carol muttered, her fingers hovering over the trackpad.

Derik raised his binoculars toward the field. "Chloe just flashed her calls," he reported. "Get anything?"

The question had barely left his mouth when a bright orange streak spiked up the screen, slicing through the blue static.

"Bingo." Carol grinned. "There's our spike—433.92 megahertz."

"What you're saying *mega hurts*." Ava frowned. "Try that again in *human*."

Carol pointed to the screen. "See this spike? That's when Max sent the signal. It's a short data burst from a low-power transmitter."

Ava blinked and shook her head. "Yeah. That helps… *not*."

"You sure it's not just someone texting?" Derik asked, scanning the sea of spectators with his binoculars. "There's like a million phones out there."

"Positive," said Carol. "Cell phones operate way higher, like in the 600 megahertz to 6 gigahertz range." She tapped the screen again. "This spike is a low-power frequency used for stuff like walkie-talkies, key fobs… simple transmitters."

Derik nodded. "I'm beginning to understand. So, Max sends a signal, and the player has some sort of receiver?"

"Yep," said Carol. "The players have some kind of device that receives the signal. We think it buzzes a certain amount of times so the batter knows what pitch is coming—one buzz equals a fastball. Two buzzes fastball inside."

"Got it," said Derik. "Pretty sad they have to cheat." He raised his binoculars, tracking Chloe. "She's cycling through her signs again."

Carol nodded, her eyes locked on the screen. She typed a quick command into the program and waited. Seconds later, a bolt of orange spiked across the display.

"Got him," said Carol, grinning like a Cheshire cat. "I've locked onto the packet header."

Ava glanced at Derik, arched her eyebrows and shrugged. "Don't look at me, I don't speak *nerd*."

"It's like the return address on an envelope," said Carol. "We know who the sender is—now we just follow the signal strength to find them."

"Oh." Ava smiled. "Like when we ran through the streets of Nantucket chasing the baddie's Wi-Fi signal. The closer we got to him, the *stronger* the signal."

"We'll know soon enough." Carol tilted the laptop toward them. "I added a little tool to help us find him."

"Or her," said Derik. "Max could be a woman."

A digital compass needle spun slowly, then gradually steadied.

"Great," muttered Ava. "More technology I don't understand."

Derik leaned forward, energized. "Alright, so which way do we go?"

"We follow the arrow. The strongest signal is coming from down there." Carol pointed into the crowd. "Someone near the front."

"Any idea what we're looking for?" asked Ava.

"A human," said Derik.

Ava thwacked him on the back of the head.

"My best guess is a walkie-talkie," Carol replied. "And they'll probably have binoculars—or a phone to zoom in on Chloe's hands and read her signals."

"Alright!" Ava said, grinning. "Let's go pay Max a visit."

CHAPTER 18
TO THE MAX

The trio split up. Derik and Carol stayed together while Ava moved down the next aisle over, cutting off Max's escape.

Carol descended the steps slowly, the blue glow of the laptop lighting her face as she hunched over the screen. "Hang on…"

The digital compass needle steadied. An orange streak shot upward, and then another.

Derik scanned the rows of spectators. "There he is," Derik said breathlessly.

He pointed to a middle-aged man in a Red Rockets cap and gray hoodie. The man leaned forward, hand dangling by his knee, his thumb tapping a button on a black rectangular device.

Carol followed Derik's gaze until she spotted Max. He looked like any other softball dad. She dropped to one knee, shrugged off her backpack, and slid her laptop inside. She zipped it, then tugged it back on.

Derik quickly fired a text off to Ava.

Row five. RR hat. Gray hoodie.

Seconds later, his phone buzzed. *I C him.*

Carol grabbed Derik's sleeve. "Zoom in—get him on video. We need proof he's cheating."

Max lifted a small pair of binoculars to his eyes. The moment Chloe flashed her signs, he checked the call band photo Aimee had sent him, then tapped out the signal to the batter.

Derik captured everything. "Got it," he said, tapping his phone.

"Perfect," said Carol.

"Now what?" asked Derik.

"Oh, the next part is easy, we're about to play wildebeest and tiger," Carol said as the crowd jumped to their feet. "Follow my lead."

With a mighty roar, the stadium came alive—air horns blaring, people shouting, the organ blasting. It was a chaotic maelstrom of noise and excitement.

Becky had struck out the last Red Rockets batter. The score stood at nine to ten in the Red Rockets' favor. This was it. The ninth inning was coming up. They had to take Max down.

Carol waited a moment for the crowd to settle a bit, then signaled to Ava to get ready.

Ava gave a quick nod-and-thumbs-up combo.

Then Carol shouted, "Hey, Max!"

A flash of surprise crossed the middle-aged man's face. He rose slightly from the bleachers, scanning the crowd, his head swiveling back and forth like a radar dish.

"Over here!" Carol shouted again, waving her arms.

Max's expression shifted from surprise to confusion. He squinted, staring hard—*Do I know you?*

Carol smiled and pantomimed holding binoculars to her eyes, then tapping her fingers against her palm.

Beside her, Derik nodded, a wide grin spreading across his face.

The sudden realization that he'd been caught hit Max like a slap in the face.

Spectators began to take notice, glancing from Carol to the bewildered man. Then, to everyone's surprise, he leapt to his feet, slamming into the man beside him, upending his popcorn and drink into his lap.

"Hey!" yelled the man, jumping to his feet, pumping his fist.

Max clambered over the row in front of him, using people's heads and shoulders for support, ignoring their angry shouts.

Ava, Derik, and Carol casually strolled down the steps to the next aisle, watching his chaotic escape unfold.

Max looked like a deer caught in headlights. He spun toward Carol and Derik, then pivoted in toward Ava. That option seemed better. No way a teenage girl was going to stop him.

Ava smiled broadly as Max tripped and fell over spectators, making his way toward her.

Derik and Carol sprinted down the stairs to the front of the stands. A six-foot walkway stretched along the base of the bleachers, with waist-high railings running parallel to the first row. Derik and

Carol split up at the bottom. With all escape routes manned, Max was not getting out.

Max reached the end of the aisle. He hesitated for half a second, then charged Ava. She sidestepped his attack easily, sending him careening into a woman's lap. He whirled back toward Ava, only to get blasted in the face with a can of hot pink Silly String.

Max clawed at his face, wiping his eyes, momentarily blinded.

"Hey!" a woman yelled as Ava snatched a giant foam finger from her hand.

"Sorry, official business," Ava snapped, smacking and jabbing Max repeatedly in the face with it.

Max stumbled on a step, lost a shoe, broke free, then bolted down the steps toward Derik and Carol.

"Stop, thief!" Ava yelled, pointing the giant foam finger as Max tried to flee.

Derik and Carol blocked his descent as he charged down the steps. Derik snatched a large lemonade from a man, and lobbed it at Max, hitting him squarely in the chest—ice and lemonade exploded everywhere.

Undeterred, Max spun on his heel to run the other way, but his escape was blocked by two security guards hurrying toward him. He roughly shoved Derik aside and rushed straight at Carol.

Ava watched in horror as the man—who was twice Carol's bodyweight—charged. He dropped his shoulder, steaming forward like a Mack truck.

Carol stood her ground knowing that the impact was going to be brutal. But at the last second, she dropped to her hands and knees, slamming into Max's lower legs. With a scream, he flew through the air and crashed hard onto the concrete.

He let out a low moan and slowly maneuvered to a sitting position. The crowd was on its feet now, whistling and applauding.

"May I?" Carol asked a mom, pointing to a half-eaten tray of greasy nachos.

"Have at 'em." The woman laughed.

Carol scooped up the nachos, and held them aloft. The crowd cheered as she brought them down over the man's head.

Breathing heavily, the security officers arrived and grabbed Max by the arms, hauling him to his feet.

"Would you mind telling me what's going on?" asked one of the officers, a man built like a cartoon superhero—massive chest, tiny legs—all he was missing was a cape and tights.

"This man is a thief," Carol said sharply. She met the officer's eyes and calmly crossed her arms. "And, since I'm a minor," she added, "I would like to speak to you about his behavior in private."

"I don't know what she's talking about," Max cried. "I was just watching the game."

"Don't worry," Derik piped in. "I have *everything* on video," he said, waving his phone.

Max's face went pale. His head sagged to his chest. It was a total *Scooby-Doo* moment. He'd been caught red-handed.

The crowd cheered as the security officers led Max away.

CHAPTER 19
BUSTED

What is she doing?

Derik adjusted his binoculars, watching the Red Rockets coach as she moved from girl to girl with a plastic bag. He shifted for a better view and saw one of the players lower her sock, pull a band from her leg, and drop it into the bag.

She's getting rid of the evidence!

Derik grabbed his phone, zoomed in, and started recording.

The head coach tied the bag shut and handed it to one of the assistants, whispering something into her ear. The girl nodded and hurried out of the dugout toward an exit.

Derik took off down the stadium steps, leapt over the railing, and sprinted through the complex and out the gate. He raced around the back of the building just in time to see the girl heading back to the stadium, empty-handed.

Coach Brier and Tina watched the video of Max sending signals in silence. The Soul Crushers peered curiously from the dugout, whispering quietly to each other.

Aimee's face was tight. She knew what was coming.

"So, explain how this worked," said Coach Brier.

"Max watched for Chloe's call," Carol explained. "He'd figure out the pitch, and then use a walkie-talkie to send signals to a receiver."

"Receiver?" asked Tina.

"According to Max, he gave the girls bands that vibrated when he sent a signal," Ava said. "They hid them under their socks."

"Well, I guess that's that," said Tina, her voice a mixture of anger and sadness. "The Red Rockets will have to forfeit."

The pulsating vein made a brief reappearance on Coach Brier's forehead. She crossed her arms and shook her head. "We're not going to win this game on a *technicality*."

She turned to the dugout, her voice filled with emotion as she looked at her battered team.

"*Fighters*," she whispered. "Every single one of them. We didn't come here to be handed a win— we came here to earn it." She turned back to Ava and Carol. "There's no way left for the Red Rockets to cheat?"

"Absolutely not," said Ava. "Max is in custody, and we have Aimee's phone."

Coach Brier allowed herself the smallest of smiles. "That's all I need to know." She turned to Tina. "Get the girls together, I'm about to give them one heck of a pep talk!"

CHAPTER 20
TOP OF THE NINTH

The Soul Crushers huddled tight, shoulder to shoulder. They were sweaty and tired, their uniforms caked in dirt, but like Coach Brier said, they were fighters—and they were ready.

"I'm not going to tell you everything right now," Coach Brier said, her voice low and steady. "But I will say this." She took a moment, meeting each player's eyes. "Whatever advantage the Red Rockets had coming into this game is gone." A slow smile crossed her face. "From this moment on, it's an even field." She let her words sink in. "Now go out there, and show me what the Soul Crushers are made of!"

For half a second, nobody moved.

Then Becky slammed her fist into her glove. That was all it took.

When the Soul Crushers took the field, something had changed. It was as if someone had flipped a switch.

Karsyn was first up. She stared down Hightower and drove a fastball straight up the middle for a sharp single.

Lilly followed with a line drive that skipped past the right fielder, sending Karsyn flying around second and into third with a slide.

Meredith stepped in, took one strike, then drove the next pitch deep into the gap. Karsyn bolted across home plate, Lilly sliding in hard behind her in a cloud of dust.

The Soul Crushers' dugout erupted—it was a two-run game.

The Red Rockets called a timeout, their coach storming the field, trying to stop the Soul Crushers' momentum.

Coach Brier met with Blakely and Kara, who were up next in the lineup. Becky and Chloe threw warm-up pitches, keeping Becky loose.

Moments later, the umpire called out, "Play ball!"

Hightower circled the mound, popping the ball into her glove. She barely let Blakely settle in before rocketing a fastball inside across the plate.

"Watch your kneecaps," the catcher joked.

Blakely ignored her, settling into her stance, eyes locked on Hightower.

Hightower circled her arm and lunged forward, releasing another fastball. Blakely leapt back just in time to avoid getting hit.

"Oops." The catcher laughed. "Close one."

The umpire stepped out from behind the plate and pointed at Hightower.

"That's enough. Knock it off. Last warning."

Hightower didn't seem fazed by the umpire's warning. She gave Blakely a thin, evil smile. She was pitching recklessly now, trying to intimidate her.

Blakely stepped out of the batter's box, settling her mind and calming her breathing. She wasn't about to be bullied. She stepped back in, cocked her bat, and got ready.

Hightower fired the next pitch, and Blakely answered by slamming a towering shot to left field. She pulled into second with a stand-up double while the Red Rockets' outfielder chased the ball down.

Kara, a massive powerhouse, stepped into the box and crouched in a wide stance, pointing to the outfield, egging Hightower on.

Hightower signaled the outfielders to play deep, knowing Kara would try to drive Blakely home.

Everyone was surprised when the pitch came and Kara dropped a perfect bunt. She sprinted toward first and dove, her fingers just touching the bag as the first baseman's glove brushed her arm.

The first-base umpire threw his arms out. "Safe."

Kara looked across the field, a huge smile spread across her face. Their plan had worked. Blakely was now in position to score.

By the time the inning was over, the Soul Crushers led by three.

CHAPTER 21
YOU'VE GOT THIS!

Becky took the mound for the bottom of the final inning, her ankle wrapped tight beneath her cleat. She threw a few warm-up pitches to Chloe and then nodded to the umpire. She was ready.

Becky felt sharper, more focused, as if the pain had narrowed everything down to a single point. The crowd disappeared—the chatter, the distractions—vanished.

She struck out the first Red Rockets batter on four pitches. The second batter lifted a pop fly that was easily caught by Meredith.

"Two outs," whispered Becky to herself. "Just one more."

Then, just like that, the next batter dropped a soft single into the outfield, and the following batter drew a walk. Suddenly, there were runners on first and second. Becky let her eyes drift up into the crowd behind the backstop. Her gaze locked with Melinda Morgan, the scout from the University of Oklahoma.

Becky's heart began to pound. It was overwhelming—ten years of her life culminating in this one moment.

The next Red Rockets batter stepped in—a lefty. She cocked her bat above her shoulder, staring down Becky.

Becky fired a fastball over the plate.

The batter answered with a screamer—a line drive straight into Becky's torso.

Becky crumbled to the ground, clutching her stomach. The runner from second dashed home and scored. Aimee, playing shortstop, scooped up the ball and fired it to Chloe at the plate, stopping any other runners from scoring.

"Time!" Coach Brier called out, already sprinting onto the field with Tina close behind. The other players gathered around Becky as Coach Brier dropped to her knees beside her.

Becky grimaced in pain, slowly rocking back and forth as tears spilled down her cheeks.

"Take it easy," said Coach Brier softly. "Take it easy. Where did you get hit?"

Becky gently touched her lower ribs, just above the abdomen. "I'm okay," she said, her voice shaking. "It just *really* hurt."

Coach Brier held Becky's shoulder, looking into her eyes. "Becky..." Her eyes dropped for a moment.

"Please don't pull me out of the game," Becky pleaded. "I've *got* this, coach. I promise."

With a grimace, she slowly forced herself to her feet. She could feel the other players—her friends—gathering around her, offering encouragement.

"I've got this," she said again, this time more firmly. She gave Coach Brier a steely look of determination.

Coach Brier was silent for a long moment—then she nodded. "Win this game."

CHAPTER 22
MAGIC

The crowd went crazy when Becky returned to the mound. Everyone was on their feet. The intensity climbed even higher when Hightower stepped up to the plate. She played to the crowd, rolling her shoulders and taking two practice swings that cut through the air with a sharp *swoosh*. She dug in and gave Becky a hateful smirk, as if daring her to throw the ball.

Becky stared at her from the mound—a long, cold, completely unbothered stare. She shook off the first sign from Chloe. Then the second. Then she gave a single, almost imperceptible nod.

She set, wound up, and fired.

Strike one.

The ball had already smacked into Chloe's glove before Hightower's bat sliced through the air.

The crowd exhaled in unison.

Becky caught the return throw and stepped back onto the rubber. Chloe flashed the sign.

The pitch came in looking like a fastball—then, at the last second, it dropped and broke sharply, catching the outside corner perfectly.

Hightower swung through it, hitting nothing but air.

Strike two.

The Soul Crushers' dugout was on its feet, white-knuckling the rail. Several players had their eyes closed in prayer. Others paced, too nervous to watch.

Becky stood at the top of the mound, the ball in her glove, completely still.

Hightower was no longer smiling.

The stadium was a wall of noise—air horns, cowbells, thundersticks crashing together, the roar of two thousand people at once. But nobody was watching anything but the battle between Becky and Hightower.

Becky closed her eyes for a brief moment, visualizing the pitch. She took a slow, calming breath, wound up, and threw. The ball left her hand in a white blur—high enough to make Hightower's eyes widen, her hips rotating, her swing already committed.

Then, as if by magic, the ball dropped—falling off the outside corner and snapping into Chloe's glove.

Strike three.

For a split second, there was silence.

Then the umpire's arm shot into the air, and the Soul Crushers absolutely, completely, and totally lost their minds.

Girls poured out of the dugout in a screaming wave, colliding with each other in a tangle of jerseys, tears, hugs, and laughter. Chloe sprinted to the mound and leaped in Becky's arms. They both went down in a heap, laughing.

Ava and Carol stood in the dugout, watching the joyful chaos on the field.

"We did it," Ava said, smiling.

"Eh." Carol smiled back. "They did it."

Ava bumped her shoulder. "We helped."

"Yeah." Carol grinned. "We did."

CHAPTER 23
WE'VE GOT YOUR BACK

Carol watched as Becky climbed to her feet in the middle of a pile of her teammates, face streaked with dirt and tears, laughing at something Chloe had said. Then she thought about Aimee, standing somewhere on the edge of all this—not quite in, not quite out. Not yet.

Aimee slowly slipped away from the celebration and headed toward the locker room. Ava and Carol followed.

When they walked in, they found her on her knees, reaching under the bench where she had hidden the phone.

"Looking for this?" asked Ava, holding it up.

Aimee's eyes widened. "What? No, why would I be looking for a phone?"

"Because it's yours," Carol said gently. "And because it has pictures of the call bands on it."

Aimee's eyes darted to the dugout room door just as it swung open and Coach Brier stepped inside.

"We know all about Max," Ava said softly, noticing Aimee trembling.

"Aimee," said Coach Brier quietly, "sit down." She put her arm around Aimee's shoulders.

The wall Aimee had been hiding behind slowly crumbled. "I'm sorry." The words came out broken, barely a whisper—then the tears came, spilling down her cheeks. She pressed the back of her hand hard against her mouth, her shoulders shaking. "I'm so sorry."

"I know you are," said Coach Brier gently. "But why? Why did you help them cheat?"

Aimee closed her eyes and took a shuddering breath. "A couple months ago I got in trouble for shoplifting—it was stupid. I was going to return it, but mall security grabbed me before I could." She shook her head, tears falling freely, dotting her dusty uniform.

"What does this have to do with the game?" Ava asked quietly.

Carol looked at Aimee. "You were blackmailed," she said gently. "Someone blackmailed you."

Aimee nodded. "Yes," she said, her voice barely above a whisper. "Darlene. Darlene told her coach."

"The Red Rockets coach," Ava clarified.

Aimee nodded again. "She told me if I didn't help their team, they would tell you. And they would tell the college scouts."

"Aimee," Coach Brier said, her voice firm but kind. "What you did was wrong, but they had no right to use that against you."

Aimee stared at her for a moment, waiting for the other shoe to drop. "What happens now?" she asked quietly.

Coach Brier was quiet for a moment. "There will be consequences. I won't pretend otherwise. But we'll figure that out together—you, me, and your parents." She squeezed Aimee's hand. "You are not facing this alone."

"Thank you," said Aimee as fresh tears spilled down her cheeks.

"For now," Coach Brier said gently, "clean yourself up and join your teammates."

Carol shifted uncomfortably near the door. They had solved cases before and usually felt a sense of accomplishment and relief, but this one felt different. Like they had won and lost at the same time.

Ava caught Carol's eye and gave her friend a small nod.

Yeah. This one was tough.

CHAPTER 24
GOOD VIBES

The cool night breeze blew across the parking lot. Thin, wispy clouds stretched across the moon; it was a perfect night for a victory. The team gathered in front of the bus, still flushed from the celebration. The photographers and the crowd had left, leaving them alone with their trophy.

"I still can't believe you guys were spying on us," said Kara, looming over Ava and Carol.

"Uhm." Carol coughed.

"I've got this," said Ava confidently. "I wouldn't call it *spying*, more like… *super-focused observation*."

"That's why you went through my duffel bag," said Karsyn, crossing her arms and narrowing her eyes.

"Yeah…" Ava said softly, suddenly losing her bravado. "About that—we saw someone handing you something at the gate."

"We thought it was a phone," Carol added.

"That was my dad," said Karsyn hotly.

"Karsyn," said Coach Brier, stepping in to diffuse the situation. "Ava and Carol were doing exactly what I told them to do."

"I still don't know why they had to watch us," said Lilly. "It's not like *we* were cheating."

"They did catch the guy stealing the signals," said Chloe. "So we owe them that."

"And even though the Red Rockets were cheating," said Tina, "you guys *still* won. That's what you should be celebrating."

"But why watch us? It's not like any of us—"

"Because of me," Aimee said, stepping forward.

"It's okay, Aimee," Coach Brier said, putting her hand on her shoulder. "We'll discuss—"

"No." Aimee gently shook Coach Brier's hand from her shoulder. Tears began streaming down her face. She turned to Coach Brier. "No… but thank you."

The silence that followed was heavy. All eyes were on Aimee as she told her story. A mixture of hurt, betrayal, and confusion swept through the team.

"You should have told someone." Becky was the first to speak. Her voice wasn't cruel, but it wasn't soft either. "You should have trusted us to help you."

Aimee's lip trembled; her eyes dropped to the ground. "I know."

Meredith broke from the group and, without a word, wrapped her arms around Aimee. Aimee went rigid for a moment, then collapsed into the hug, sobbing.

Carol and Ava stepped back, watching as, one by one, the team joined in, wrapping Aimee in one giant hug.

"Gross," whispered Ava, backing away.

From across the parking lot, a lone figure made his way toward the girls. As he passed beneath a light, he tossed his head to the side, his bangs swishing across his forehead, revealing a gleaming blue eye.

Carol waved him over.

"Everything okay?" he asked, eyeing the girls, many with tears running down their faces.

"Yeah." Carol smiled. "I think so." She draped an arm over Derik's shoulder, then immediately backed off. "What is that smell?"

"Oh, ahem—yeah, that." Derik smiled. "First, thank you for noticing. Second, I had to do a bit of dumpster diving to find the transmitters. That's how devoted I was to this case."

"One second." Carol lifted the bottom of her hoodie and pulled a small vial of golden liquid from her crossbody bag. "Here." She sprinkled some onto Derik's hoodie.

"Sheesh," Derik cried out. "Not so much."

Ava snorted, and leaned in for a sniff. "You smell like flowers and hot dogs." She sniffed again. "With a hint of mustard."

"Great," said Derik. "Just what I was going for."

"You turned everything over to the officials?" Carol asked.

"Yep, I gave them the transmitters. The Red Rockets coach and assistant coach have been put on leave pending an investigation, and the team has been moved to last place."

"That's horrible," said Ava. "All to win a game."

"What's *horrible* is cheating," said Becky, joining them. She sniffed the air and gave Derik a suspicious look.

"New deodorant," he muttered under his breath.

"Those coaches tried to steal our future from us," said Becky with a little heat in her voice. "Many of us have been playing softball since we were six years old. We worked hard to get where we are."

"You're not wrong." Ava nodded. "You guys played amazingly well, despite everything stacked against you."

"And with a hurt ankle and a line drive to the gut," Carol added.

"Yeah." Becky nodded. "It was a lot." She narrowed her eyes and leaned in, examining their faces. "I can't believe I didn't recognize you two." Becky laughed. "I used to babysit you guys."

"We are professionals." Ava smiled.

"What about the scout?" asked Carol. "I saw her in the stands with her little radar gun."

A huge smile crossed Becky's face. "You mean Melinda Morgan?"

"I guess…" said Carol.

"She offered Chloe and me *scholarships* to play for the Oklahoma Sooners softball team." Becky's voice was absolutely giddy with delight.

"Of course you turned her down," Ava teased.

"Yeah, I told her that I knew two kids that desperately needed babysitting."

"Long-term employment." Carol laughed.

"But seriously, guys, thanks for your help," Becky said, smiling. "I'm not sure we would have won without you." She wrapped her arms around Ava and Carol in a tight hug.

Becky turned to Derik, who responded with his trademark hair swish, cracking her up.

"I guess you deserve a hug too." She reached out to pull him in, then suddenly shot backward.

"I knew it. I'm repulsive," Derik groaned.

Becky laughed and offered a fist bump. "You guys make a great team. And believe me," she said, smiling, "I know a great team when I see one."

DON'T MISS OUT!

Join the adventure at avaandcarol.com and be the first to know about upcoming *Ava and Carol Detective Agency* mysteries.

I hope you had as much fun reading this story as I had creating it. If you have questions, ideas, or just want to share your thoughts, don't hesitate to drop me a note at thomaslockhaven@gmail.com. I would love to hear from you!

If you enjoyed the story, I'd greatly appreciate it if you could leave a quick rating or written review. Your feedback not only means a lot to me, but it also helps other readers discover my work.

OTHERS BY THOMAS LOCKHAVEN

AVA & CAROL DETECTIVE AGENCY

Book 1: The Mystery of the Pharaoh's Diamonds

Book 2: The Mystery of Solomon's Ring

Book 3: The Haunted Mansion

Book 4: Dognapped

Book 5: The Eye of God

Book 6: The Crown Jewels Mystery

Book 7: The Curse of the Red Devil

Book 8: The Witch's Secret

Book 9: The Christmas Thief

Book 10: The Mystery of the Egyptian Pyramid

KIDS MURDER MYSTERY CLUB: COLD CASE PODCAST

Join Ava, Carol, and Derik in the *Kids Murder Mystery Club* as they take on chilling cold cases that refuse to stay buried. From long-forgotten murders to secrets hidden deep within their town, each case pulls them further into danger.

With their podcast as a guide, the trio follows clues, uncovers hidden truths, and faces suspects who will do anything to keep the past buried.

Every case is a puzzle. Every answer comes at a cost.

Can they uncover the truth… before it's too late?

RIPLEY KOOL AND THE INVESTIGATORS

Meet Ripley Kool, Gilly, and Alexis—three best friends with sharp minds, big imaginations, and a knack for solving the strangest mysteries in town. From vanishing dinosaurs to treasure-hunting parrots, no case is too weird, wild, or wacky. Packed with laughs, suspense, and nonstop sleuthing, this thrilling series will have you guessing until the very last clue. Are you ready to open the next case file?

S.M.A.R.T.

They may be just middle schoolers, but they're not your average kids. As Team Kaboom, they conquered the Mastermind Competition, and now, there's a secret they're hiding: they've become the FBI's ultimate weapon against crime!

CALISTA CHASE TIME SLEUTH

Time-traveling Calista Chase faces swashbuckling pirates, treacherous seas, and the mystery of Blackbeard's treasure in a thrilling adventure where history and legend collide. Join her in an adventure where survival is the ultimate challenge!

Book 1: The Deadly Cavern
Book 2: The Screaming Mummy
Book 3: The Chalice of Souls

Join Tommy, Eevie, and Drew on their heart-stopping adventures, where danger lurks at every turn. Prepare for mind-bending puzzles and thrilling escapades that will leave you wanting more.

Learn more about Thomas Lockhaven's other books by visiting the webpage: twistedkeypublishing.com/author-thomas-lockhaven